INSURANCE
SECRETS
REVEALED

RODGER NELSON

TREBOR & TAYLOR

Copyright © 2002 by Rodger Nelson

Legal Disclaimer
This book contains the author's views and opinions acquired through experience in the field under discussion. It is sold with the understanding that the author and publisher are not engaged in rendering any legal, financial, or other professional services through the publication hereof. This book is intended as a general overview of the subject matter hereof and only should be used in such manner. Specific issues pertinent to the reader's particular situation should be referred to the appropriate professional. Therefore, if legal or other expert assistance is needed, the services of a competent professional should be sought. Some of the information presented in this book is not applicable in all states or to all Insurance Companies, and may be current only up to the date of printing. Therefore, this book should be used as a general guide and not relied upon as the only source of information in regard to the subject matter covered.

The author and publisher shall have neither liability nor responsibility to any person or entity with respect to any loss or damage caused, or alleged to have been caused, directly or indirectly, by the information contained in this book.

First published by Trebor & Taylor Publishing Co., Inc.
P.O. Box 145 Flossmoor, IL 60422-0145

ISBN 0-9721048-0-1

Library of Congress Control Number: 2002106860
Manufactured in the United States of America

First Printing, November 2002

I am forever grateful to the creator for giving me life, and the chance to share my experience, knowledge & compassion with the rest of the world. This book is dedicated to my wife, children and family, all of whom play such an integral part in making life worth living.

Rodger Nelson

INTRODUCTION

Why You Need This Book...

My reasons for writing a book such as this are varied. First and foremost, my compassionate nature has played a purposeful part. After spending years as an insurance agent for a Fortune 500 insurance company, I have seen quite a bit during my career in the insurance business. A lot of what I have witnessed, however, has been to the disadvantage of the average insurance buying consumer.

Nonetheless, it is my goal to share with you many tips, techniques and "secrets," that will not only empower you, but will save you money as well. A publication of this sort has been needed, as consumers everywhere have lacked the ability to be informed, educated and more importantly, put on a level playing field when dealing with insurance companies and their agents. And with today's skyrocketing insurance rates, discovering ways to save money has never been more important.

The goal of this book is to uncover some of the most beneficial "inside" information, for the most popular types of insurance sold by insurance agents, as well as, to offer my years of experience, condensed into the most important tips and rules every insurance buying consumer should know. The "secrets" presented in this book are considered as such, because they represent information not always commonly known to the average insurance buyer. I can honestly tell you that there are millions of people who buy insurance every day, only to walk away with inadequate protection, often due to a salesperson's or agent's lack of knowledge, experience, and/or concern to advise them properly.

More importantly, insurance companies are in business to make a profit and *may not always volunteer to you ways to save money!* If I had one "weakness" as an agent while working for my former employer, it was my desire to be honest with my customers and look out for *their* best interest, as opposed to meeting the demands of my superiors, which was often, all in the name of profit. This is yet another reason why there is such an increased need for accountability to the public.

Lastly, we are in the midst of a period of enlightenment. We are an information-hungry society who needs to be educated, informed and empowered more than ever before. All one has to do is observe, look at our nation's Enron and Worldcom scandals as evidence. What you have before you is an opportunity to learn "inside" information that some would rather you not know. Please take the time to absorb these *insider* tips, tricks & "secrets" that I've learned over the years, and wish to share with you. Finally, be sure to refer back to this informative book as necessary, you'll be glad you did!

Warmly,
Rodger Nelson

CONTENTS

CHAPTER 1

THE ART OF
MAKING A PROFIT:
AN AGENT CAUGHT
IN THE MIDDLE

n today's climate of corporate scandals, financial wrongdo-
ings and political chaos, one can only ponder the future
state of affairs in America. Not surprisingly, after we dis-
sect, analyze and offer some sort of rationale for what occurs,
we usually find greed to be the common denominator in each
case. When insurance companies lose more money than they
care to, the usual solution is to either increase insurance rates,
limit the specific type & amount of coverage on a policy, or
worse yet, stop offering the coverage in question altogether.
When one observes the "landscape" more attentively, it can be
seen that one way to deal with areas that an insurance company does not care to offer insurance in, is to put a limited
amount (if any), of agents in those particular areas. This can
greatly limit the amount of insurance sold in a particular re-
gion or area by a specific insurance company, as most people
will call (and prefer) an agent or insurance company that is
nearby. Could this be why a lot of insurance companies do not
have a presence in inner cities or urban areas? Albeit, like so

many other things in our society, it's a case of: don't tell people they can't have something, just don't make it easily accessible.

As an agent, there were times when I was asked to provide reports concerning profit, which would require a certain percentage of customers to fit within certain "boundaries." These boundaries were basically pre-determined percentages of how much of the general public should fit into a certain category. Like most insurance agents, I was responsible for making the company a profit, and was held accountable for a lot of "objectives."

For instance, I was often told that only so many people should be rated as driving to and from work, and only so many people should be entitled to certain discounts (statistically). So, if 8 out of 20 people told me that they only drive their vehicles for pleasure, here I was caught in the middle, between giving the customer an accurate quote (relying on the honesty & integrity of the customer) and satisfying a predetermined objective which would result in the company making more of a profit. I was held accountable for a *lot of things*, even the frequency of when the company's customers had accidents, clearly something that a lot of agents felt was unfairly beyond their control. I raise these points to say: "there are some things that are beyond your control as a consumer, however, there are also many things that you could control *if only you knew about them*."

Another point that I want to make is regarding payment options. Insurance companies, as well as a lot of other companies, prefer that you have your payments automatically deducted from a checking or savings account. Statistically, its been shown that a person's payment is more likely to be made (on time) this way, keeping the business "on the books."

However, it was suggested to me to tell my customers that this was the *only* method of making monthly payments, (even though it wasn't), especially when it came to life insurance.

Secret: You see, life insurance is very profitable for insurance companies, it usually pays the highest commissions for agents and in most cases, more of an effort is made to keep a life insurance policy from canceling, compared to most other types of insurance policies.

I was always afraid that if I told people that the only way to pay on a monthly basis was to have their payment automatically deducted from a checking or savings account, I would find myself in trouble, if and when the customer found out this wasn't the case. So, despite the urging of my superiors, I continued to honestly give people options. Perhaps the insurance business wasn't the best fit for me. Don't get me wrong, I had an office full of plaques, awards and other accolades that I'm very proud of. However, being the honest and compassionate person that I am, made it hard for me to try to squeeze every ounce of profit out of my customers. And, (because of this), I often found myself nervously trying to defend my position when discussing "profitability" with my superiors.

Secret: When considering whether or not a person's insurance was to be cancelled due to his or her claims history, I was told to consider the payment history of the customer, and whether or not the customer was a "problem customer," or in no uncertain terms, someone who's policy was always canceling for non-payment. Being an "insider," it didn't take me long to realize what I had heard from people on the "outside" all along:

Insurance companies are clearly interested in people who don't have claims. As soon as you start to have multiple claims, you're no longer considered to be "profitable" for them to keep you as a customer. I would hear this cry for concern time and time again from customers who were suddenly "dropped" from insurance companies after having a few claims, despite being a "worry free" customer, faithfully paying their premiums for many years. (In some cases, as much as 20 years or more).

Clearly, one of the problems with this industry is that consumers need a way to become empowered. How can people speak up about certain practices and issues, when they don't know that such practices and issues exist in the first place? Think about it, the average person shopping for insurance has to rely on the integrity, professionalism and expertise of the insurance person making the sale. In my opinion, this may work fine for other industries. However, insurance is way too serious a topic to not at least have a working knowledge, or better yet "the inside scoop," as to what's really going on. Within the pages of this book, I have tried to convey both "the inside scoop," as well as some of the basics that everyone should know to look out for their own best interest.

CHAPTER 2

WHAT YOU SHOULD KNOW ABOUT *YOUR* AUTO INSURANCE

DOES YOUR INSURANCE COMPANY MEASURE UP?

For the sake of familiarity, I will begin this chapter with auto insurance, otherwise known as Casualty insurance. Insurance companies generally come divided into two categories: preferred and non-preferred companies. You will find that preferred companies usually deal direct with consumers, are generally more selective about who they insure, and are perceived by many as being more reputable overall.

On the other hand, "non-preferred" or "substandard" companies usually offer insurance through insurance brokers and generally have more lenient "qualifying" guidelines. *Secret*: Many people that I have come across were under the impression that these brokers were actually insurance companies. To the contrary, they are basically middlemen who place insurance through carriers whom they have a contract with to represent. In some cases, the broker may also have its own insurance company to refer its customers to, however, this is rather the exception than the norm. Additionally, a lot of people learn first-hand, the hard way, that some of these so called "substandard" companies do not always deliver the type of service (especially with claims), that you expect from an insurance company. Furthermore, they may have a lower, allotted rate per hour, that they will pay repair shops to fix your vehicle. *Secret*: This means that you may have to take your vehicle to lower quality repair shops, whose hourly rates coincide with how much the substandard insurance company is willing to pay, unless you're willing to pay the difference out of pocket, to take your vehicle to a more reputable (and higher quality) shop. *Secret*: Some repair shops don't accept repair business from substandard companies for fear that the substandard insurance company will not pay the repair shop the going rate for the covered repairs, and/or may not pay for the claim/repairs in a timely basis. Substandard insurance companies are usually a viable alternative for drivers with a driving history that would make them ineligible for preferred carriers, and for drivers who may not have had any prior insurance (at least for the most recent 6 or 12 months).

Insurance companies are normally rated using a grading system similar to that which we see in our school system (A-F etc), with an A++ Superior being the highest ranking. One of the most well-known and respected authorities on insurance company rankings is a company by the name of A.M. Best. Their web address is www.ambest.com. In addition, your state should have its own Department of Insurance, which can offer information pertaining to an insurance company's complaint ratio, overall customer satisfaction, and its history of claims resolution, for any insurance company operating in your state. *Secret*: In many cases, the rate that I was able to offer a potential customer (from the preferred company that I worked for), was cheaper than the rate, which the customer had gotten from a substandard insurance company. This meant that I was able to offer them a *rare* combination of better quality service at a lower price.

INSIDE "TRICKS" OF INSURANCE PROFESSIONALS

When buying automobile insurance, however, don't always accept the lowest price as being the best way to go. Like the old saying "you get what you pay for," this is also true when it comes to your insurance coverage. *Secret*: Many insurance agents will give you a quote using the lowest possible limits of liability (ex. 20/40/15 displayed on your policy and/or quote), in order to be more competitive with other insurance companies on price, particularly in over the phone quotes. However, in this case, you the buyer would potentially suffer from not knowing that all coverage(s) are not adequate for most people, and will often walk away with inadequate protection. Have your agent or representative explain the coverage limits and offer alternative quotes with higher limits of liability, to increase your protection from personal lawsuits, in the event that you find yourself liable in an accident. *Secret:* Most of all, don't allow people to sell you insurance using a "cookie cutter" approach. Each individual's needs are different and should be treated as such!

Secret: Some insurance agents will automatically classify you as a driver, as driving for pleasure, instead of to and from work, in an effort to give you a lower quote to earn your business. However, while this may save you some money initially, you may be surprised later when the insurance company "reclassifies" you as driving to and from work and not for pleasure. Consequently, you would then receive a new policy & higher premium, based on your "new" classification. *Secret:* Many consumers are then perplexed about the higher rate, because they know that nothing has changed on their part, other than the fact that they were initially given a discount, that unbeknownst to them, they did not "qualify" for in the first place. I have seen this happen to people and this would cause them to become irate, having no clue, as to why their insurance rate had increased.

WHAT ALL THOSE NUMBERS REALLY MEAN...

It's amazing how many people have no idea what their auto insurance policy really covers. When you see numbers like: 25/50/25 at the top of your policy or quote, these are your limits of liability, meaning that if you're at-fault in an accident, these are the maximum limits payable on your behalf, by your insurance company. The first number 25 (meaning $25,000), indicates the maximum that the company will pay for each person who sustains bodily injury in the accident. The second number 50 (or $50,000) is the maximum that the company will pay for the total damages of the accident. The last number 25 (or $25,000), is what the insurance company will pay for property damage or to fix vehicles/property etc. on your behalf, if you're found to be at-fault in an accident or collision, or even not at-fault in certain instances, when you must submit a claim through your own insurer.

Some states allow lower limits (20/40/15). However, these limits are not considered to be an adequate level of protection. Furthermore, it is generally recommended that you purchase higher limits (50/100/50 or 100/300/100), or even higher for better protection. More importantly, if you're a homeowner and/or have larger assets that you own, you will certainly want to have the highest amount of liability coverage that you can afford. The extra liability would certainly help to protect you in the event that someone decides to sue you for being liable, for various types of accidents and/or bodily injury. *Secret*: Much to the surprise of most consumers, the liability portion of an insurance policy is usually quite inexpensive, in relation to other coverage(s) that you'll find on your auto or homeowner's insurance policy etc. Overall, increasing your liability coverage is a low-cost way to get the added benefit of extra protection. I would always inform people that they could increase the liability portion of their auto policy for only pennies per month difference. And, in most cases, that's exactly what they did.

THE POLICY: THINGS EVERY DRIVER SHOULD KNOW

Secret: There are a lot of people who are driving around with the absolute lowest limits of liability allowed by their state. Good insurance agents refer to this as "garbage coverage." Limits of 20/40/15 for example, are just not adequate, especially when you can purchase much higher limits at a relatively cheap cost difference, as stated above.

The truth of the matter is that there are insurance people who will sell you limits of 20/40/15, because they know that their rates are high. They will offer you the absolute lowest coverage, which usually means their lowest rate, in hope that you will buy insurance from them. *While doing so may save you a few dollars, they really are not offering you adequate protection, and after all, isn't that why you're buying the insurance in the first place?*

Secret: People have come to me after buying insurance through brokers, and had discovered that these brokers had placed the liability portion of their auto policy with one insurance company, and the comprehensive & collision portion of their policy with another insurance company. I refer to this as a'la carte coverage, and it is often more confusing for consumers to keep up with. There was one particular instance where a client who came from another insurance company, thought that he had full coverage auto insurance, and actually had only liability insurance. And, I'm sure it was because of how his auto insurance policy was separated between two different carriers. The bad thing about this case is that this gentleman had no clue that he was driving around with only liability insurance. A lot of consumers prefer to have all of their insurance (auto, home etc.) with the same carrier, let alone having their *auto* insurance policy divided between two different insurance companies.

HOW AN AGENT'S OR SALESPERSON'S LACK OF KNOWLEDGE AND/OR CONCERN AFFECTS YOU!

It warrants repeating: One of the main reasons that you want to *empower yourself* is because you could be buying insurance from a sales representative that lacks the proper knowledge, experience or concern to advise you properly. It's important for your agent or representative to at least *offer you alternatives* and *let you make the decision as to whether you want to purchase higher or lower limits of liability/protection, and/or additional options*. Unfortunately, in a lot of instances, this is just not done and can potentially cause you some serious hardship.

Secret: In most cases, when you lease a vehicle, the limits of liability are required to be higher, for example: 100/300/50. These limits are often required to be higher because the leasing company still has a major interest in the vehicle, and wants to make sure that you have enough coverage to protect both you and them in the event that you have an at-fault accident. Remember to consider this when reviewing the monthly cost on a leased vehicle, as this requirement may cause the cost of your insurance to be somewhat higher. Also, see the section on Leased Gap Insurance later in this book.

Secret: Speaking of payments, here's a common misconception that a lot of people have about insurance payments... Some insurance companies will require a large down payment from you to start your car insurance, then, they will tell you that you pay for 4 months and you'll receive the last 2 months free. Are you really getting free insurance? NO, not at all, your down payment included the payment to cover these 2 "free" months. So don't be misled into thinking that you are getting free insurance. Few things in this world are free and insurance certainly isn't one of them. People would always ask me if they were entitled to 2 "free" months, and much to their surprise, I would explain to them how this "marketing concept" works.

The second item usually listed on an auto insurance policy will be for Medical expense. When an accident occurs, this coverage will usually cover all reasonable expenses (within usually one year of the accident), for necessary medical services, ambulance, hospital and funeral expense, up to the specified amount on your policy. *Secret*: If your vehicle is equipped with an air bag, you should receive a discount on the *medical* portion of your policy. More importantly, you will often need to ask about many of the discounts mentioned in this book to save money. *Unfortunately, in many cases, such discounts will not voluntarily be offered to you.*

THE BASICS IN PLAIN ENGLISH

Comprehensive - this portion of your policy will normally cover the cost to repair or replace your vehicle, if it sustains damage from hail, vandalism, wind, fire, flood, explosion, falling objects, glass breakage, riot, civil commotion, collision with birds or animals and if your vehicle is stolen. Normal wear and tear would not be covered under this category. Some people have a car that they only drive during the spring and summer months and will keep their vehicle garaged the rest of the year. If you keep your vehicle garaged for a specified period of time, you may want to consider having only Comprehensive coverage on that particular vehicle, during the time it stays garaged. Comprehensive coverage can protect your vehicle for covered losses that could occur while your vehicle is being stored. Upon driving the vehicle again, be sure to add full coverage insurance on your policy (i.e. liability, collision & comprehensive etc.)

Secret: If you get a chipped windshield as a result of a rock or piece of debris hitting the windshield, let your insurance company know. There might be coverage for this under the comprehensive portion of your policy. You may be able to have the hole or crack repaired without paying a deductible.

However, if you wait to act, what started as a small hole can eventually turn into a widely cracked windshield, requiring a full windshield replacement. Vehicle glass repair shops have indicated to me in the past that a small tiny hole is repairable, and a crack that is no wider than a dollar bill can often be repaired. However, if larger, a full windshield replacement may be necessary.

Collision - This portion of your policy will cover the cost to repair or replace your vehicle, if you or a covered driver was involved in an accident with another vehicle or property. If your insurance company is paying to fix your vehicle, you will have to pay your "deductible," which is the amount that you, the *customer*, is liable for, once the work on your vehicle has been authorized and completed. In fact, in most cases, when an insurance company is paying out money on your behalf, expect to pay a deductible.

Secret: Hitting a pothole that causes damage to your car should normally be covered under your collision coverage.

Uninsured Motorist Coverage (U.M.) - This coverage protects you, the insured, or anyone in your insured vehicle, for bodily injury caused by a hit-and-run driver, a driver of a stolen vehicle, or for injury caused by any driver legally liable who has no insurance.

Underinsured Motorist Coverage (U.I.M.) - This coverage can provide for bodily injury, if you, the insured, or someone riding in your insured vehicle is injured, and the other vehicle's driver does not have *enough* insurance to cover you and your passenger's bodily injury damages. *Secret:* As a rule of thumb, both U.M. & U.I.M. coverage(s), should *at least* have the same limits as your bodily injury/liability limits mentioned earlier, and obviously for good reasons.

Death and Dismemberment (D&D) - You can use this endorsement to inexpensively add coverage for damages, which result in death, dismemberment of a limb, or loss of sight etc., to either you and/or a passenger in your insured vehicle. *Secret*: This coverage is a good value and should pay, in addition to any amount that is also collectible under medical expense.

Communication Device Coverage - This coverage can pay for the theft or damage of your Cell phone, CB radio and other communication equipment in your vehicle at the time of a "loss."

Uninsured Motorist Property Damage (U.M.P.D.) - This endorsement is useful when there is only liability coverage on your vehicle. UMPD allows you to have your vehicle repaired up to a certain dollar amount, if the at-fault party that hit your vehicle does not have any liability insurance. In a nutshell, if you already have full coverage insurance, you shouldn't need this endorsement. *Secret*: This coverage is not always automatically added and should be requested if desired; it is relatively inexpensive and *highly recommended* for those who only have liability coverage. Many of my clients would state: How having UMPD was almost like having full coverage, and for just a few bucks a month. (In my opinion, a best-kept secret!)

There is one so called "catch," regarding whether or not Uninsured Motorist Property Damage (UMPD) will cover you: You are normally required to obtain the information of the responsible driver who has hit your vehicle. This would be the driver's and vehicle owner's name, address, plate no., and driver's license number etc. *So, Uninsured Motorist Property Damage coverage will usually not apply in a hit & run incident, where the identification of the at-fault owner or driver is unknown.*

Emergency Road Service (or E.R.S.) - Having this "endorsement" will reimburse you as the insured for expenses incurred, if your covered vehicle breaks down and you have to have the vehicle towed, get a flat tire and/or need road side assistance (i.e., needing to jump start a dead battery or running out of gas etc.). This coverage is usually provided on a reimbursement basis. Basically, you would pay a tow truck driver first, and then, show your receipt to your insurance agent or representative, so that you can be reimbursed for your out-of-pocket expense. I was always able to reimburse my customers "on the spot." Insurance companies differ on how much they will reimburse you; it's usually an amount between $50 and $100.

Secret: This (ERS) coverage is not always automatically added and should be requested if needed. *Secret*: I would encounter many clients who told me that they belonged to a city or state motor club, which, for about $80 a year, would come to their rescue if they were stranded. My reply to them was that for about $12 a year, they could have the same type of coverage with the insurance company and save themselves some money. Be sure to ask your insurance representative, up to what amount can you expect to be reimbursed for an Emergency Road Service claim. Additionally, many new car warranties include this coverage as part of the vehicle's warranty program. *Secret*: Consequently, you may not need this coverage on your "new" vehicle and should make sure that you're not paying for this coverage unnecessarily.

If you have two vehicles and one is covered for emergency road service under a vehicle warranty and you have a second, older vehicle, without emergency road service, you should consider adding emergency road service to the older vehicle on your auto insurance policy. Adding this relatively inexpensive coverage is a good idea, since, with the older vehicle, there is more of a probability that you will require roadside assistance and/or emergency road service while driving it.

Secret: Just so you're aware, when you file an emergency road service claim, it becomes a part of your claims history, just as if you were involved in an accident. However, this sort of claim is not normally looked upon the same way (negatively), as if you had an at-fault accident, unless you have had so many road service claims, that your insurer interprets such claims as being "excessive" and threatens to cancel your policy.

Rental Reimbursement - this coverage will pay for reimbursing you for the cost to rent a car in the event of an accident or theft. Don't rely on this "optional" coverage being added automatically, be sure to ask for it if you want it, and look over your policy when you receive it to make sure that it was included. *Secret*: I have observed auto policies where the limit for this coverage is only $20 per day for a rental, the customer, *not knowing that higher limits were available,* accepts this limit, much to their opposition later. Consequently, you may choose to purchase higher limits such as $30, $40 or even $50 a day, if you think that you would like to rent a more expensive vehicle at the time of a "loss."

Secret: What I have noticed some consumers do is request a $20 to $30 day limit, and *if* they are involved in an accident, at *that* time, they have the option of paying the difference of a higher amount in order to drive a more expensive rental vehicle. This is a money-saver. On average, the most that you would be able to keep the rented vehicle would be for 30 days. Hopefully, that should be enough time for your vehicle to be repaired. *Secret*: If a repair shop has taken more time (to fix your vehicle) than the maximum time allowed for you to keep your rental, your insurance company or the repair shop may be able to "work something out," to cover the additional expense that you would normally have to pay, for the time that the rental vehicle was in your possession.

Secret: Usually, if a vehicle is stolen, most reputable insurance companies will offer their insured a rental, *regardless of whether or not this coverage was included on the policy.* Lastly, be sure to ask in the event that your vehicle is stolen. A common misconception about rental reimbursement that some people have, is that this coverage will pay for you to have a rental car if your vehicle has to go to the repair shop due to a normal maintenance issue (such as a transmission failing or other mechanical "wear and tear" problem). This (in most all cases) is simply not true. When an insurance company reimburses you for the use of a rental vehicle, it will most likely be in conjunction with a claim filed on your behalf.

Sometimes, an insurance company may have a good relationship with a local car rental company that will allow you to rent a car without paying for the costs initially, while waiting to be reimbursed from the insurance company later. In this case, the car rental company will bill the insurance company once the vehicle is returned.

Secret: I also want to mention that in some states; there is a certain amount of time (for example 48-72 hours), after a car is stolen, before the insurance company will authorize the use of a rental vehicle at their expense.

GETTING THE MOST OUT OF YOUR INSURANCE

Secret: Are you aware that you may be able to lease or purchase a car through your insurance company with good results? Some insurance companies that offer financing, can provide information as to dealer cost and special incentives, in an effort to help their customers get the best deal possible when buying or leasing a new or used vehicle. *Secret:* I've known of cases where the finance department of an *insurance company* helped prevent their customers from being ripped off by car dealers, by providing the customer with enough "inside" information, to help the customer get the best deal possible on a new vehicle.

TIPS ON KEEPING YOUR RATES DOWN

Secret: If you have had one moving violation within the last three years, it may or may not be held against you (depending on the insurance company). If your state has a Traffic Safety School Program, definitely consider attending. Keep in mind, there is usually a slightly larger fee for attending the class as opposed to pleading guilty and not attending.

However, successfully attending the class usually means that the ticket should not be reported on your motor vehicle record (which most insurance companies check), and can help keep your auto insurance rates in check. Another option given by most states would be for you to pay a fine and basically plead guilty, with the ticket reported on your driving record. *Secret:* I have known many insurance rates to *double,* just because drivers had one ticket too many. This "situation" could have been avoided, had these people known of the consequences involved, from having an "extra" ticket on their driving record. There is talk of late, of having traffic safety school available online, which would certainly be a great convenience for a lot of people. *Secret*: Remember, the extra time and effort on your part (by going to Traffic Safety School), can save you BIG money on your insurance premiums, by helping to keep your driving record clear of moving violations.

Secret: If you get a ticket for speeding 20-25 miles per hour over the speed limit and that ticket stays on your record, you may have to pay **twice** the normal amount of insurance, with a company that would have given you their best rate, had you had only one ticket, and that ticket was for speeding only 10-15 miles-per-hour over the speed limit. Beware, I have known of cases where a driver had only one ticket, but because it was for *excessive speeding* (for example, **20-25** miles-per-hour over the speed limit), the driver had to be placed in a *high-risk* (rates twice as high) category, which was just as expensive as having an **at-fault accident!**

Higher deductibles mean lower monthly payments and lower deductibles result in higher monthly payments. Typically, you save more money over the long run by having a higher deductible such as $500, compared to $250. However, for some, it may be difficult to "come up" with $500 as opposed to $250 at the time of a loss or accident. Therefore, each individual is obviously going to have to determine what's best for his or her situation. *Secret*: You should be able to change your deductible at anytime, not just at your renewal as some may have you believe. And, with regards to insurance expense, I want to caution you that a two-door vehicle will typically cost more to insure than a four-door version of the same vehicle. Keep this in mind when looking to buy your next vehicle.

Secret: Let's say that you had auto or homeowner's insurance with a company, and during that time you had an at-fault auto accident, moving violation, or a relatively large homeowner's claim (over $1,000 for example). If you let your insurance cancel, especially for a specified length of time (i.e. 90 days or so), your insurance company may require you to go through the application process all over again, (basically treating you like a new customer), *with the claim now being held against you and causing your rate to increase dramatically.*

Secret: I have known of some big name insurance companies that have technically looked at their customers in a "different light," once their customers' insurance policies cancelled. These companies basically made people's driving record an issue, when it wasn't an issue prior to their policies canceling. This reminds me of some credit card offers that I've gotten in the past. The credit card company basically offered me a low interest rate to entice me to get the credit card. However, should I ever pay late (i.e., 30 days after the due date), then my rate would dramatically and permanently *increase*. At least in the case of the credit card, I knew *up front* what was going to happen, having had the opportunity to read the fine print.

INSURANCE COMPANIES CAN DIFFER, OH SO GREATLY!

Not all insurance companies have the same quality of claims service. Therefore, if another insured hit your vehicle, and that person is with a "non preferred" or "substandard" company who's claim service may be questionable, (I'll show you how to check this out later), you may be better off with allowing your company to handle the claim, especially if it looks as if the other driver's insurance company is giving you a hard time, and/or does not want to admit to the fault of their insured.

At least you should know what type of service you can expect from your own insurance company. In this instance, you normally will pay your deductible, which could later be recouped by your company from the other insured's company, or attempted to be recouped from the other driver, if the other driver or vehicle owner did not at least have liability insurance.

Ask your insurance company if they will guarantee the work done on your car, if done by one of their authorized repair shops. *Secret*: What a lot of insurance consumers don't know, is that if you're not completely satisfied with the work done on your car, you should not have to accept it as being completed. Part of your decision to purchase a lot of things, could have been the fact that they came with a guarantee. Why wouldn't you expect the same from a repair shop that is fixing your car after an accident or fender bender?

WHEN ACCIDENTS HAPPEN

When involved in an accident or other incident regarding some type of loss or damage, it is usually required by insurance companies that you have a police report. Having a police report can benefit you in more ways than one. *Secret*: When an insurance company finds a claim on your driving record, they may see that you were involved in an accident. However, the insurance company's report may not indicate who was *at fault*. By having the police report, you have documentation, which can help show an insurance company that an accident was not your fault. *Secret:* Make sure the report you show your insurance company is called the **Crash Report** (official police version), and not the Motorist Report (initial driver version).

Secret: Always keep additional copies of the crash report. If you no longer have the crash report, you should be able to obtain a copy from the police headquarters in the city, state or town where the accident occurred. The crash report can usually be obtained within a week or two after the accident for a nominal fee such as $5.

When you're involved in an auto accident, it's best to notify the police and your insurance company as soon as possible. This may sound like common sense, but let me give you an example of what can happen if you don't (because a lot of people fall victim to this scenario). Scenario #1: Let's suppose that John gets rear-ended by Mike, both John and Mike get out to inspect their vehicles, neither sees any obvious damage and both Mike and John agree to just "forget about it" and go on their way. However, later that day, John starts to experience some neck and back pain and decides to contact his doctor, insurance company, attorney and the local police. Start to get the picture? Now, all of a sudden, we have an accident reported that makes Mike look like a hit & run driver. My point here is to notify the proper authorities.

Secret: If you are involved in an accident, which is clearly *not* your fault, given that the other party is with a good insurance company, you should consider filing a claim *directly through the other insured's carrier*. This can benefit you in two ways:

1. You should not have to pay a deductible amount.
2. You avoid involving your insurance company and having a claim (even though it's not your fault), on your record.

Secret: Let's consider scenario #2 to illustrate what I'm referring to: Lisa and Kim are involved in an auto collision, and the accident was clearly 100 percent Lisa's fault, because Lisa ran the red light. Let's assume that reputable, preferred companies insure both Kim, and Lisa. If Kim files a claim with her own company, not only does she have to pay her deductible for her claim, but now she has a not-at-fault accident on her record. If she files her claim with Lisa's company, not only does she NOT have to pay her deductible, but this claim should be on Lisa's record and NOT Kim's. These above two scenarios represent a few things that most people may not be aware of, because no one ever told them until it was too late!

Secret: This is yet another reason to have a police report. Insurance company reports may show that a person was involved in an accident, however, may not show if the person was at-fault or not. The burden of proof will be on the person to prove that the accident was not his or her fault, in order to get the best rate possible. This is where the police/crash report can come in handy (showing the outcome of the accident).

Secret: If you were previously insured with a substandard company, be aware that some of these companies do not report your claims history to the "database," that other insurance companies get their information from, when checking for prior claims on your driving record. Therefore, a preferred insurance company will not have readily available access to your prior claims history and will most likely contact your previous, substandard insurer for additional information.

On the other hand, if you were previously insured with a preferred carrier, you may be asked by your "new insurer," to show a recent "renewal letter," bill, or proof of insurance card. In particular, a renewal letter shows that your prior insurance company was willing to renew your insurance, and that you have had insurance for the past year or six months. Most *reputable* insurance companies do report to the "data base," mentioned previously. Any claims and tickets that you may have had while insured with them will most likely be accessible via a "claims" and Motor Vehicle Report (MVR).

If you are buying insurance from a preferred company, and were previously insured with a non-preferred or substandard company, you may be asked to sign what is called a "Disclosure of Authorization," or a "Letter of Disclosure." This is a document that your "new" insurance company will send to your prior insurance company, asking your prior insurer, how long you have had insurance with them, and if you have had any claims during that time.

Buying insurance could be more expensive if you do not already have insurance; your "new" insurance company has no way of checking your most recent driving record, since you have not had insurance prior to them insuring you. You could have been involved in numerous accidents, and it would be difficult for your "new" company to find out about any claims during this period (since you had no insurance at the time). So, basically, your new insurer would charge a higher rate for insuring (what they deem) a potentially higher risk (you). After purchasing insurance with your new company at a higher rate, you may have to keep the higher rate for 6 months to a year, after which, you should qualify for a "preferred" status, providing that you have not had any at-fault accidents or moving violations during this "trial" period, and you still meet the "qualifying guidelines" for their preferred rate.

On your auto insurance policy, you will most likely see the term: "symbol," which is a way that insurance companies place a value on your car. This predetermined "value" helps the insurance company determine the amount that your car is worth for rating purposes.

Secret: Often, the same vehicle may be assigned a different symbol. You may have an upgraded edition. For example, a car may come as a base model LE, then the next level up could be an SE, and the highest level could be an SLE. As far as symbols go, the agent may have the choice of choosing multiple symbols for your vehicle: 19, 20, and 21, with 19 resulting in a lower insurance rate than 20 or 21. This will also help to determine the value that the insurance company will place on your car at the time of a "loss." Consequently, if your vehicle was totally destroyed, you should expect to get more for your vehicle if it had a symbol of 21, compared to a symbol of 19.

Secret: In cases where clients of mine had expensive aftermarket equipment on their vehicles, I would ask them how much this additional equipment was worth, and increased the symbol on their policy, which (accordingly) placed a higher value on their vehicle. This is another good reason why your agent should see your vehicle if possible. If there is no mention of special, added equipment on your policy, your insurance company will likely, *not cover* the equipment at the time of a loss, because in their opinion, they were not aware of the added equipment and subsequently, did not collect premium (money) for it.

Another factor regarding your auto rate would be how your insurance company classifies you as a driver. A driver that drives for pleasure will generally pay less for auto insurance than a driver who drives 15 miles one way to work. Other factors affecting your insurance rate could include your age, marital status, where the car is kept, your driving record, prior claims or accident history, how many policies you have with the insurance company, the type of vehicle, whether you're a student (with a good grade point average) and the list goes on and on.

Secret: There is a relatively new technology that is helping insurance companies properly classify drivers by revealing all of the licensed drivers in a particular household. This report comes via computer and helps the insurance company properly charge a rate, based on any other drivers that might live in your household and potentially drive your vehicle. Why? Insurance companies want to know if other drivers exist in your household, who warrant a higher premium because of their age, or driving record etc.

In a nutshell, insurance companies feel that since these other drivers pose a higher risk, the premium that you pay should be based on the assumption that these other (risky), drivers may drive your car. With most reputable companies, anyone that has permission to drive your car and has a valid driver's license is usually covered, therefore, the insurance company may want to know about all of the potential drivers, so that they can base their premiums (your rates) accordingly. This way, if something happens (i.e., an at-fault accident etc.) they will feel that they have collected the proper amount of money from you, for the risk involved.

Regarding claims, most reputable companies should have a list of preferred repair shops that they "work" with, and who they know do good work, which should be guaranteed. *Secret*: If you have a newer vehicle, it's a good idea to ask your agent/representative, what's his or her company's policy on replacing parts on newer vs. older vehicles. Some companies will use only authorized manufacturer's parts on vehicles no more than three years old. Other companies may differ on this policy, some may not use original equipment at all, you'll just have to ask. *Secret*: Although, most good insurance companies have a list of preferred repair shops, if you have a body/repair shop that you would like to take your vehicle to, let your agent or claims department know. Some companies will allow you to take your vehicle to the repair shop of your choice.

Lastly, some insurance companies offer mechanical breakdown insurance. This coverage offers protection for your vehicle against: you guessed it, mechanical breakdown. If you find a company that offers this coverage, you should find out what (specifically) will be covered *before* you buy. By all means, *read the exclusions;* doing this will tell you what's **not** covered, that way, you can avoid getting surprises later. Furthermore, many people have called their insurance company to file a vehicle or property claim, only to find out that there was no coverage in the insurance company's policy for their "loss."

During my career, I have talked to people whom had several of these "claims," reported on their claims history report. *Secret:* In each case, *the insurance company did not offer any coverage or pay out any money, however, still reported the person's "inquiry" as a "claim filed."* This not only seems unfair, but has caused many people frustration, especially when they were eventually cancelled by their insurance company for excessive claims, and/or went to obtain insurance coverage from a different insurer, who subsequently denied offering them insurance due to their prior "claims history."

Basically, if it is a question of whether or not any coverage will be provided for a particular loss or incident (such as a vehicle or property claim), caution should be exercised when contacting an insurance company. In my opinion, especially in instances such as these, I would rather talk to an agent first, who can advise whether one would benefit from filing a claim, and then allow either the agent to file the claim, or, after it is known for sure that a loss will be covered, call an insurance company's claims department or claims service center. The usual response of these claims service representatives is to report every inquiry as a claim filed, and unfortunately, consumers don't find out that their inquiries are reported as claims until it adversely affects them later.

Finally, as I've uncovered quite a bit in these beginning pages about auto insurance and the claims process, remember, when talking to your insurance company or agent, be sure to ask as many questions as possible.

CHAPTER 3

YOUR HOME...
PROTECTING YOUR
MOST VALUABLE ASSET

Homeowner's insurance policies can differ greatly from company to company. It is a good idea to ask your agent or representative for a replacement cost quote, in addition to whatever other quotes you may obtain. *Secret*: In some cases, insurance companies may offer lower price brackets if you insure your home anywhere between 80-100 percent of replacement cost (which is the estimated cost to replace your home in the event of a total loss).

For example, a policy that covers your home for $100,000 will normally provide an additional 50 percent of that amount for your personal property. Rounding out the picture will normally be 100,000 in liability coverage, which protects you from lawsuits if someone is hurt on your property, or your pet hurts someone etc. *Secret*: The amount of liability on your homeowner's policy can be increased to $300,000 for a relatively inexpensive amount (compared to the amount of extra protection that you get). This difference could be as low as $10-$12 a year. Your policy should also have coverage for other structures such as a garage, which will usually be an additional 10 percent of whatever your home (or dwelling) is insured for. An average policy will provide $1,000 for emergency medical coverage, should someone get hurt on your property and require quick medical attention. Again, this is another coverage that can be increased (usually up to $25,000), relatively inexpensively.

Thus, an average homeowner's policy may include the following:

Coverage A	$100,000	Dwelling
Coverage B	$50,000	Personal Property
Coverage C	$100,000	Personal Liability
Other Structures	$10,000	Garage
Other	$1,000	Medical

The amount of coverage for a property (listed as Coverage A-Dwelling) on insurance policies will normally increase by small percentages annually, in an effort to keep up with inflation. This increase along with an increase in the company's rates can make an insurance premium out of reach for some people. I have known this to be the case particularly with seniors on a fixed income and younger married couples just starting out. *Secret*: What you may not know is that you can normally request to have your homeowner's dwelling coverage reduced in an effort to save money on the premiums you pay. While this is not the ideal thing to do, it may be the only choice for some people, as opposed to allowing their coverage to "lapse out" or cancel totally, due to their inability to pay.

Secret: Most homeowner's policies will pay for your living expenses if you have to temporarily move out of your home due to a covered loss, such as a fire, storm damage, explosion etc. On average, you would have up to 12 months of living expenses paid during this period. Additionally, if you rent out a portion of your house to a tenant etc. and normally collect rent from that tenant, most policies will pay you what you would normally (and reasonably) charge your tenant to live in your home. Basically, despite having to temporarily relocate, you would continue to collect your rental income from the insurance company, until your home was restored back to a habitable condition.

Secret: Another great feature included on some policies, will pay for the loss of refrigerated products, in the event of a power loss (rain storm etc). People always thought that this was great to have on their policy, especially due to the fact that they didn't have to pay a deductible if something happened. A normal "pay out" under this type of coverage would be anywhere between 250 and $500.

When buying home insurance, you should consider some relatively inexpensive optional coverage(s) such as personal property replacement cost, increased liability, increased coverage for jewelry, watches, and furs etc. These optional coverage(s) are well worth the extra premium for the additional protection that they provide.

An example of personal property replacement cost (covered in more detail later) would be, for example: If you purchased a television set and paid $600 for the set when it was originally purchased. If afterwards, someone broke into your home and stole the TV set, an insurance company would normally determine the value of the set and pay the full value minus depreciation, since the TV was considered used at the time of the theft. With personal property replacement cost, the insurance company should offer you payment for the TV as being brand new, or whatever the cost to replace it with a new one. Which could be either the exact same brand and model with the exact same features, or payment to purchase a new one with like and similar value. *Secret*: If you have this coverage added to your homeowner's policy, keep in mind: Most insurance companies have a clause which states: if they pay you for a personal property replacement cost claim (i.e., you had personal property replacement cost coverage), you must actually *replace the property* to receive full replacement cost, if you don't replace your "lost" property, the insurance company has the right to pay you the *depreciated value* for your property instead.

Secret: Some insurance companies are looking at a person's credit as a condition of whether or not they will offer the person insurance. Of main concern to these companies could be previous bankruptcies, foreclosures, repossessions, collections and judgments etc. According to some insurance companies, there has been a strong correlation between a person's prior credit history and their propensity to file a property claim.

An insurance company may want to review your credit history before you actually obtain the insurance, so keep this in mind when you're closing on a home and your loan officer/mortgage company wants to check your credit record a final time before you actually close. Additional inquiries on your credit report can lower your score, fortunately, most mortgage lenders don't consider this to be a big deal, allowing it to affect your closing or refinance loan.

As some insurance companies consider a person's credit history when purchasing homeowner's or renter's insurance, there are sometimes, provisions allowed that will enable those with past credit problems to still get approved. *Secret*: Insurers that take credit into account may offer customers the opportunity to take a credit course or seminar, with insurance being given, contingent on the customer successfully completing the credit counseling course.

Secret: As an additional incentive for completing this type of course, you may also be entitled by law to add a positive personal statement to your credit report, and your name may also be included in a database to inform lenders that you have successfully completed a formally recognized credit education program. If you've had past credit problems, which were due to a medical condition, be sure to let your insurance company or agent know. In many cases, your credit problems may not be held against you, *if* the "problems" were due to medical illness etc. This may or may not be evident when a insurance company checks your credit report, so be sure to mention it if necessary.

Secret: There are certain things that you should obtain from your insurance agent or representative, which are required by most mortgage lenders, before they will allow a closing to take place:

1. Proof of insurance - Be sure to get a copy of the **Declarations Page.** This is usually a one-page summary of coverage(s), which shows the property address, how much the property is insured for, who the mortgage company, insured and insurance company are, the yearly premium and the effective dates of coverage. Agents normally fax this to your lender, however, be sure to get a copy for your personal records. You should be able to obtain this directly from your agent's office.

2. Proof of payment - Be sure to get a copy of the receipt showing the effective dates and the amount of money paid by you for your homeowner's insurance. Sadly, many insurance agents and sales representatives lose their jobs for misappropriating company funds; having a receipt can benefit you in more ways than one.

3. Be sure to get a copy of the homeowner's insurance application from your agent, and take copies of all of the above documents with you to your closing. These requirements are usually faxed to your loan officer;

however, it's a good idea for you to have copies as well, for back up purposes. I have noticed some people will literally wait a day before a closing (or even the same day), to purchase their homeowner's insurance. In a lot of cases, this is just not a sufficient amount of time for all involved, as most agents will have to visually inspect a property before they will insure it.

When closing on a home, you will most likely be asked to pay for the first year of insurance up-front and in full. This is because the mortgage company does not already have an "escrow" account to pay for your insurance since you are just purchasing the home. After having made your mortgage payments throughout the first year that you own your home, the mortgage company should have funds set aside, which are taken from your monthly payments, to pay your homeowner's insurance premium for the *following year*. *Secret*: Be sure to find out at your closing, if your homeowner's insurance will be escrowed (accounted for in your monthly mortgage payments), or if you will have to pay for it out-of-pocket yourself.

Be sure that your insurance agent obtains your mortgage company's "mortgage clause," prior to you closing on or refinancing your home loan. This "clause" is usually obtained from your loan officer or loan processor and basically details how a mortgage company wants their name listed on all insurance documents. This is very important, even for a new mortgage lender that you may have, as a result of refinancing your loan, or if your mortgage loan was sold. *Secret:* I have known of many cases where a person refinanced, or their loan was sold to another lender, and neither the person (insured), nor lender, notified the insurance company to update the company's files with this "new" information. As a result, the insurance company's bill for the customer's insurance went to the "old" mortgage company (not the new one), resulting in the customer's policy being cancelled for non-payment. This type of miscommunication can cause you a lot of grief and frustration, particularly if your homeowner's insurance was canceled and you had a claim or loss during that time. Hopefully, if this were to happen, a good, reputable company will take responsibility for such a mishap. Finally, make sure that your insurance company is notified whenever your mortgage company has changed!

Secret: I have known of insurance agents that were fired for stealing money. Their former customers would come to me for help, stating that they paid particular agents money for homeowner's insurance, however, never received a policy. What these agents did was collect money from unknowing customers, and did not turn in the applications or money to their employer. The employer became aware of this "situation" when several customers called the company to report a homeowner's claim, and quickly discovered that there was no official record of these people having any homeowner's insurance.

Since most of these customers had copies of applications signed by the agent, with effective dates of coverage, and the amount paid for the insurance, the agent's company honored the customer's claim. If a customer had no copy of an application, receipt, cancelled check or other proof of payment, his case would be much harder to prove. This type of thing goes on more than you would imagine. This is also why insurance companies look into the financial background of a person wanting to become an insurance agent. If a person cannot manage their own personal financial matters (i.e., poor credit history etc.), it only makes since that they may have trouble managing someone else's (the insurance company's) money.

Toxic Mold: Nature's Hidden Health Threat

Mold is a serious health problem today and can cause various health ailments such as: nosebleeds, headaches, sinus infections, chronic fatigue and even short-term memory loss. Mold usually grows in damp places including: behind walls, under floors and above ceilings. Around the country, mold growth has reached dangerous levels in many schools, forcing some to close altogether.

Insurance claims for mold are consistently increasing, as more and more homeowners file claims for mold. In some cases, the amount of mold has been so extensive, that complete homes have been destroyed, forcing insurance companies to cut back on their coverage for mold and water damage. Recently, in the state of Texas, several insurance companies have implemented plans to drop mold coverage from their homeowner's policies.

My first experience with dealing with mold involved one of my clients who called to say that her son was experiencing nosebleeds due to the mold in her home. After filing a claim and upon further investigation, I found that the company that I worked for had no clear cut process for dealing with mold claims, only to state that each situation will be dealt with on a case by case basis. This reminds me of how a lot of insurance companies handle rarely chartered territory that has reached epidemic proportions. The normal protocol seems to involve cautiously paying for claims when legally obligated, while asking for permission and support to either raise rates or eliminate coverage altogether. Interestingly, this seems to occur just at the point when consumers are in need the most.

If you suspect mold in your home, don't hesitate to contact the proper authorities, starting with your insurance company. A lot of information can be obtained about mold on the Internet. Listed below are some websites that you may find helpful concerning mold:

www.epa.gov/iaq/pubs/moldresources.html
www.cdc.gov/nceh/airpollution/mold/links.htm
www.moldupdate.com

A key factor in controlling mold is to eliminate sources of moisture and condensation. Proper clean up after flooding and/or water damage is also a necessity in helping to prevent mold growth. Ask your insurance agent or sales representative if water damage coverage (such as flood insurance or sewer back-up coverage) is extra. Sewer back-up coverage will protect your personal property, flooring, appliances etc., from water damage, backing up through the drain opening (usually) in a basement floor. Flood insurance, on the other hand, can cover damage to your home when the *community* is flooded, resulting in inside and/or outside damage to your home and personal property.

Flood insurance is administered through the Federal government; however, it should be offered and obtainable through your insurance representative. Your lender should inform you if flood insurance is required for your property *before you close on your home. Secret*: Flood insurance and sewer-back up coverage (although both protect against water damage) are two distinct and separate types of coverage(s) and should not be confused with one another. I have talked to many people who had to be educated on the difference. And, keep in mind, that both flood insurance and sewer back-up coverage are usually *optional* coverage(s), and not automatically included in a typical homeowner's policy.

Insurance companies may offer you a quote to insure your home at full replacement, which is good and recommended. This "replacement cost" is the insurance company's calculated estimate of what it would take to "replace" your home, in the event of its total loss or complete destruction.

However, I do want to point out that if you live in a sound, masonry (brick) structure, the event of a total, complete loss to your property (although possible), is not as common, as with vinyl, frame and other more combustible types of homes.

Secret: For Condo-owners, who have an Association, check to see if you're required by your Association Bylaws to cover only the interior of your unit, or the interior *and* exterior etc. Knowing this will determine, in great detail, how your homeowner's insurance policy should be structured. You may be liable for (only) your floor coverings; interior drywall etc., *or* you may be responsible for your immediate exterior walls and roof. Each association is different and your responsibility as a homeowner should be made clear to you.

For the record, both renter's and Condominium Unit Owner's insurance are classified as different types of homeowner's insurance. *Secret*: Generally speaking, as with auto insurance, the more that an insurance company wants to see your property, check your prior claims history and take pictures of your home, is usually a good sign that the company may have good claims service. If the insurance company knows that they are going to pay a claim fair and square, they also want to know that they're not taking on an *existing* "problem," before the insurance policy has even been made effective.

Secret: Some insurance agents will only sell you a renter's insurance policy if you have other "types" (i.e. auto or life etc.) of insurance with the agent or company. Their "philosophy" is that a renter's insurance policy may average $125-$200 a year in premium, however, you, the customer, may get (for example) $25,000 worth of coverage for your personal property. That's a lot of coverage & value for $125-$200 dollars per year. Since these agents are responsible to their companies for making a profit, they have to find a happy medium between how much money is made for the company, and how much money the company has to "pay out," based on the amount of claims in their "book of business." In other words, he or she wants to make sure that the company has a reasonable chance to make a profit off of you (i.e., with multiple lines of insurance), compared to the company having to pay a relatively large amount of money to you, in the likely event that you had to file a large renter's claim. Furthermore, agents usually get bonuses for making a profit.

It's a good idea to mention to your insurance agent or representative, any additional needs you may have. For example, you may have a home-based business and need certain "endorsements" (specifically designed coverage(s) to meet a certain need), to protect certain equipment, business personal property in your home, or increased liability, as would be needed in the case of in-home child care providers. *Secret*: You should also mention if you have done recent renovations to your home. Doing so, may result in additional discounts, as well as making sure that your home is adequately covered. For instance, if you've just added a $4,000 wooden deck, increase the coverage on your home by $4,000, so that your deck will be accounted for, in the event that it was destroyed along with your home in a fire etc.

You should also ask for discounts for a professionally installed and monitored security/fire alarm system, if you have one, as well as a discount for membership in a formal neighborhood watch program, if one exists in your area.

Ask about discounts for having dead bolt locks, smoke alarms, and fire extinguishers, if you have them or plan to purchase them. *Secret*: In an effort to save money, consider choosing a higher deductible (ex. $500, $1,000). Unlike automobile insurance, in a lot of instances, for a homeowner's claim, an insurance company can subtract the deductible amount from the proceeds payable to you, once your claim is settled.

However, if a third party is involved, such as a contractor (needed for repairs), the insurance company will normally pay for any authorized repairs minus your deductible, in which case, you would be responsible for paying your portion (deductible), directly to the contractor.

When purchasing your home or even afterwards, consider buying mortgage protection insurance. This coverage (which is essentially life insurance), can pay for the remaining balance of your mortgage in the event of the death of you and/or your spouse. *Secret:* In a lot of cases, the death benefit in these policies is structured to decrease as your mortgage decreases over time. A regular life insurance policy can accomplish the same thing, without a decreasing death benefit. A marketing ploy that some will use, is to present this type of (mortgage life), insurance as something other than "regular" life insurance. Savvy insurance salespeople will lead you to believe that you need both, when a fully adequate, "regular" life insurance policy can accomplish the same thing.

Secret: **Be extremely careful** when buying life and/or mortgage protection insurance through direct mail, TV or other media (i.e. credit card offers etc.), offering to pay off your mortgage in the event of death. A lot of these offers will pay only in the event of ACCIDENTAL death, and some people find this out after it's too late. This is why a physical, or doctor's visit, is not normally required as part of the policy application process, in some cases. Because in these cases, your health is not a factor, since the policy will only pay if death results from some type of accident etc. Accidental death coverage is usually relatively inexpensive and can be used to help *supplement* a life insurance policy that will pay under any normal covered circumstance. It should be added as an *addition* to regular life insurance, instead of being the only form of life insurance that you have. *There is no guarantee that anyone's death is going to be accidental.* Finally, you should be able to purchase Accidental death coverage as a low cost endorsement to your regular life insurance policy.

For most of us, our home will be the biggest purchase of our lives, so don't skip when protecting this most precious asset. *Secret*: When something happens that results in you filing a claim through your insurance company, consider whether filing the claim is worth it financially (i.e., if the claim amount is considerably more than your deductible), for you to receive the compensation, while putting a claim on your record. Of course, this is why we buy insurance. However, insurance companies have underwriting "guidelines," in regards to the amount and/or frequency of claims that are allowed before they cancel a homeowner's insurance policy. My point here is that, you want to use your insurance when you really need it, and not for every "minor" incident that may occur on your property. This especially holds true for people with lower deductibles (usually $250 or less), when deductibles are relatively low, most people will be enticed to file a claim, because they will not have to pay much out-of-pocket. Finally, as with other insurance policies, the higher your deductible, the lower your premium will be and vice versa. However, you'll find that over the long run, you'll save much more money with the higher deductible. However, be sure to choose a deductible that you can afford to pay at the time of a loss. For this reason alone, (despite paying more in the long run), some people will prefer to stay with lower deductibles.

Secret: It is a good idea to keep a record of your personal property. This could mean photographing, videotaping, keeping receipts, keeping your bill of sales and getting an appraisal for your jewelry. This "inventory keeping" can definitely come in handy if needed during the claims process. Some insurance companies may even have a personal property inventory pamphlet, or brochure, that they can give you, to record whatever personal property you may have.

Other points to consider: some insurance companies will not insure you if you have certain types of pets, others may consider your credit worthiness, most will definitely consider the condition of the house (is it well maintained? any damage to the dwelling and exterior, including sidewalks?). Some companies may require you to already have homeowner's insurance before applying for it with them. Regarding pets, more and more companies are not insuring homeowners who have dogs such as Pit Bulls, Rottweilers, German Shepards, Chinese Chows or Wolf Hybrids. Statistics tell a grim story of how many claims are being paid, as a result of vicious dog attacks, mostly to children.

When you have to file a homeowner's claim (as with auto insurance), your insurance company may have a list of preferred contractors that they use on a normal basis to do repair work. This does not necessarily mean that you can't use your own contractors, only that the contractors on the company's preferred list have demonstrated a proven track record for customer service, have passed the insurance company's eligibility process and will most likely guarantee their work.

Secret: In general, most insurance companies state that if you have had renovations done to your home, which at least add up to $5,000, you should notify the company so that they can adjust/increase the coverage on your homeowner's policy accordingly. This "adjustment" will compensate for the additional renovation, because your home will most likely be more valuable as a result, and you will certainly want your home covered for its new "value." I have known insurance companies to actually mail out a survey/questionnaire to their customer (homeowner's) base. This type of questionnaire was basically used to get an update on the value of the homes that the company insured. Questions were asked pertaining to: Whether or not the homeowner had done any new improvements, how many bedrooms and bathrooms the property contained, the square footage, and ceiling height etc. By using this survey, the insurance company could attempt to actually determine the correct replacement cost, and then offer customers the option of insuring *at* replacement cost, which, in addition to more coverage for the homes, would also result in higher premiums and more profit for the insurance company.

Secret: In addition to this type of survey, an insurance company may also hire an independent third-party company to go out and physically inspect your property from the outside, and report back to the insurance company: The property's approximate square footage, whether or not the property appears vacant, if there is evidence of any vicious dogs on the premises, and the overall condition of the property. *Secret*: Insurers realize that some properties they insure, may potentially be either underinsured, or over-insured, and may contact you to see if they can persuade you to change your coverage. Even without any changes authorized by you, you may notice that your overall dwelling coverage (coverage A), increases in relatively small increments on a yearly basis. The reason for this is so that the insurance company can keep up with the cost of inflation, should they have to pay a homeowner's claim for your property, in any given year.

Safety Secret: Some insurance companies frown upon barbecuing on a wooden porch or stoop, because a lot of fires are started this way. Also, having circuit breakers instead of fuses is preferred. There are also cases of people using pennies (be cause they're made of copper) in place of fuses when a fuse is blown. This practice has also caused a lot of fires to homes and is **not recommended**. For modern homes, you are much better off upgrading to circuit breakers if you currently have fuses. With all of the electrical appliances that most people have today, fuses don't handle the load as efficiently.

Secret: A home with brick exterior will normally have a lower premium than a home with vinyl, aluminum, wood, etc.

This is because brick is not as combustible. As stated earlier, a total loss is less likely to occur to a sound brick home, compared to one that is made of vinyl, aluminum or wood etc.

Secret: Finally, if insurance companies are declining you, make sure you get the reason for being declined in writing. I remember hearing my superiors telling agents to make sure they send out a Letter of Declination, documenting the specific reasons why a person was denied insurance. My superiors were (understandably) concerned, that a person could try to sue the company for discrimination, or a practice known as "Redlining," (where insurance companies decline people based on where they live), if no official documentation were given, as to the reason why the person was being denied insurance. *Secret:* Whether you are approved or not for homeowner's insurance, should be based on the merits of the actual property, and the legal underwriting guidelines of the insurance company. A person may also be denied insurance if their property is in some type of area that poses an environmental hazard, or is not suitable for residential use.

Don't despair, if you have been turned down by several insurance companies, your state may have a "plan" set up for homeowners like yourself to get insurance. These rates are usually higher and the coverage may not be as in-depth. However, this certainly beats not having any homeowner's insurance at all. It's worth mentioning again, some of the reasons that you may be declined homeowner's insurance from an insurance company, could be the condition of your property (including garage), your credit history, the type of pet or dog that you have and your prior claims history, to name a few. These situations are deemed to be higher risks by most insurance companies. Be sure to consult your insurance company, and agent, for guidelines specific to you and your state.

CHAPTER 4

THE HIGH PRICE
OF INSURING
YOUR HEALTH

Health Insurance is usually more expensive to purchase individually, compared to buying it through group plans (as offered by most employers). Some insurance companies, even multi-line insurers that sell auto insurance, offer a "PPO" plan, which stands for Preferred Provider Organization. PPO's are perceived to be more flexible than HMO's, allowing you to go to any doctor, without normally requiring a referral from your primary physician. *Secret*: Some people have explained their dissatisfaction with HMO's, stating that when it's necessary to make an appointment to see their doctor, they feel that they encounter more of a "hassle" (i.e., discouraging the use of the doctor's time, unless the situation is perceived by the doctor's staff as being medically urgent), compared to the same process with a PPO.

A typical PPO plan might cover all major medical expenses, inpatient and outpatient surgery, and some in-home care. In addition to allowing you to go to any doctor, the insurance company will often pay a higher percentage of the total medical expense, if you go to one of the doctors in their "network."

Secret: Among the things that you may see *"excluded"* in an average health insurance policy, could be any of the following:

1. Pre-existing conditions
2. Medical services, treatment or supplies, which are not considered medically necessary (such as weight reduction), or which are considered experimental (unless otherwise covered)
3. Cosmetic surgery, unless required due to a covered injury, or congenital defect in a child, covered under the health policy from birth
4. Vasectomies, tubal-ligations, and other procedures to prevent conception
5. Drugs or medicines, which have not been approved by the United States Food & Drug Administration
6. War or acts of war that result in injury or death
7. Injury or sickness resulting from having committed a felony
8. Intentionally self-inflicted injuries, or attempted suicide
9. Alcohol and/or drug abuse treatment
10. Treatment and services etc., to help you stop smoking

Secret: Look for a good health policy that may include additional benefits, such as coverage for: Mammograms for women, (with frequency and type most likely dependent upon the age of the woman) and Preventative Medical and Wellness Care, for which you may not have to pay a deductible, co-payment or coinsurance amount (explained on the following page). Note: Be sure to read your particular health insurance policy, for specific information on limitations and exclusions that pertain to you and your state.

In most cases, you will have to satisfy your yearly deductible before the insurance company starts to pay for any covered costs. Once your deductible has been paid, you might have to pay a "coinsurance" amount, which is an amount over and above your deductible. Coinsurance is basically an amount in which you, the insured, pays a smaller percentage (usually 10-20%), of a total predetermined amount (also known as a corridor), while the insurance company pays the difference.

The coinsurance amount may be somewhere between $5,000 and $10,000. To illustrate how this works, let's assume that you've paid out-of-pocket to meet your deductible, then, out of the next $5,000 to $10,000 (coinsurance amount), you would then pay 20 percent. Let's also assume that your deductible is $500, and for illustration purposes, the coinsurance amount is $5,000. This would mean that your total out-of-pocket expense would be $1,500 for any given policy year. That's the $500 deductible, plus 20 percent of the $5,000 (i.e., $1,000 for coinsurance).

After this amount has been satisfied, your insurance company would normally pay 100 percent of any covered illness *beyond this point*. The insurance company requires these coinsurance and deductible amounts, to have you share in the cost of the covered expenses, much like a homebuyer shares in the cost of their mortgage loan by contributing a down payment. Your "Maximum Benefit," is usually a lifetime benefit and can range anywhere between 1 million and 5 million dollars or higher. Some health plans will offer dental, vision and maternity coverage(s). However, these coverage(s) are often excluded. If you have a pre-existing condition, this type of condition may also be excluded. You must check with your health insurance provider to know for sure. When looking for health insurance, it's worth checking around, as some companies are more lenient as far as who they will insure compared to others.

Secret: There are also temporary health insurance policies available, usually, anywhere up to six months consecutively. These policies can cover you while in-between jobs, or, if you do seasonal work and need health coverage during the "off-season." These policies are also relatively inexpensive compared to regular health insurance. I have been asked the question: Can this temporary policy be renewed? Technically, in some cases, with at least a one day gap in coverage, meaning, after the initial policy ended, you can have it reissued for an additional six months, depending on the company. This technique would basically allow you coverage for a full year, minus the day or two that the policy was out of force. Normally, this policy may only be in force for a six-month term, and can only be reissued one consecutive time. However, be sure to check with your insurance company and state laws for guidelines applicable to you.

As Americans get older, more and more people are purchasing Long Term Care insurance. This coverage will help cover the cost of expenses to care for the elderly and those beyond a certain age, whom require special care. *Secret*: Similar to life insurance, this coverage should be purchased while you are in relatively good health, to avoid any issues of uninsurability at a later date, due to health reasons. This means that if you have a pre-existing condition, the insurance company may decline to issue you a policy, when you could have possibly purchased the policy *prior* to the oncoming of the (now) existing condition. See the upcoming section on Long Term Care for more details.

Secret: Another consideration is that some insurance companies may offer you (as their insured) a chance to purchase additional coverage for such things as experimental cancer treatment. There is usually an additional premium for adding this coverage. However, this coverage can pay for "experimental" treatments as they are developed, in an effort to improve the condition of those inflicted with life threatening illnesses such as cancer.

Secret: If you favor a particular company's health policy, and the policy does not include dental and vision coverage, there are inexpensive "supplemental" plans that you can purchase (through other companies) which offer dental and vision coverage, to help you in obtaining a "complete" health care package. Finally, have your insurance agent or representative provide you with what's called an "Outline of Coverage" for your review. This "outline" will explain in more detail, which conditions are covered and which are excluded in your health insurance policy.

A Word About Medicare

People aged 65 and over are normally entitled to receive Medicare Part A (Hospital Insurance), without having to pay a premium, because either they or their spouse paid Medicare taxes while employed. Medicare is divided into two parts. Part A consists of Hospital Insurance and Part B consists of Medical Insurance. Part A will help pay for inpatient hospital care, some home health care, hospice care and some skilled nursing facility care. Part B will help pay for outpatient hospital care, some home health care (that Part A may not cover), and doctor's services. Basically, Part B will help pay for "eligible" covered services when they are medically necessary. If you find that you need to purchase Part A, you can call the Social Security Administration toll free at: (800) 772-1213 or contact your local Social Security office.

Opposite Medicare, a Medigap policy can provide coverage for things that Medicare does not cover. You can purchase a variety of plans (A through J), with A having the least benefits and J having the most. *Secret*: If you purchased a Medigap policy **after** 1990, your policy should automatically renew each year *as long as you pay your premiums*. If you purchased a Medigap policy **prior** to 1990, your state may have had laws (at that time), which allowed insurance companies to *not* make these plans guaranteed or automatically renewable. *Secret*: Medigap policies normally do not cover vision or dental care, long-term care, private nursing and unlimited prescription drugs. If your insurance company goes bankrupt or no longer offers Medigap coverage through the Medicare program, you should be able to buy plans A, B, C, or F, that are sold in your state. *Secret*: You must apply for these plans no later than 63 days after your coverage ends.

Secret: Be informed, that an insurance company can't deny you the insurance coverage or place stipulations on when the policy can start. *The insurance company shouldn't charge you more premium, due to your past medical history or any current health conditions that you may have.* Additionally, your insurer should cover you for all pre-existing conditions. Lastly, it is illegal for someone to sell you a Medigap policy when any of the following occur:

A. You already have one

B. They claim that a Medigap policy is part of the Medicare Program or any other Federal program.

C. They know that you are enrolled in either a Private Fee for Service Plan or Medicare Managed Plan.

If you suspect illegal activity, you can call either Medicare at (800) 633-4227 or your state's Insurance Department. See the directory toward the end of this book for a list of State Insurance Department telephone numbers.

CHAPTER 5

THE UNTOLD "*SECRETS*" OF LIFE INSURANCE

There are in general, three common types of life insurance. They are: Term, Universal and Whole Life. When comparing the three, Term life insurance is normally perceived to be the cheapest, with all other things being equal. Term offers protection in the event of death, however, does not build any cash or "cash value."

Another point to remember about term insurance is that at some point your premium will increase (usually, every year, 5, 10, 15, 20 or even 30 years etc.). *Secret*: Term insurance may start out being the cheapest of the three, however, I have known of many instances where it proved to be more expensive in the long run, due to its predetermined, future increases.

Secret: Term insurance is often referred to as providing "temporary" protection for several reasons. In the case of a policy designed for "mortgage protection," the death benefit may continue to decrease to a point until it eventually turns to zero. This is called a "Decreasing Term Policy." Basically, the concept with this type of policy is that you take out enough insurance to cover the balance of your mortgage upon your death.

As you live in your home over the years and your principal mortgage loan amount decreases, your mortgage life insurance death benefit also decreases and basically keeps pace with your declining mortgage balance. Once your mortgage loan is paid in full, your decreasing term policy approaches a zero death benefit. A term policy may also reach the end of its duration before a whole life policy. Where a whole Life policy might end at age 100 or your death (whichever comes first), a term policy may end at 95 or even as early as 75. The other point to remember is that term insurance will increase at scheduled intervals, where whole life premiums (although starting out higher) should remain the same throughout the duration of the policy.

Secret: Look for a good term policy to offer a feature called: Guaranteed Renewability, meaning that once you've qualified for a life insurance policy and it's issued to you, the policy will be guaranteed to be renewed at regular intervals, without you having to "qualify" again by taking additional physicals etc. As mentioned previously, at some point, all term insurance policies normally increase in price. You may find that after you've purchased your policy, the price of the policy will stay the same for 1, 5, 10, 15, 20, or even 30 years, followed by increases based on your age at specified intervals. People will often purchase term because of its cheaper price and are often told to: Buy term, and invest the money that you save (from not buying universal or whole life) in some type of investment vehicle.

Secret: During my career, I would always hear statements like this from people who *only sold term* and didn't have the option of selling universal or whole life insurance. So, in my opinion, these people were biased to begin with. *Secret*: With specified increases, and no build up of cash value, *you could find yourself paying much more for the term insurance policy in the long run*. The interest rates on universal life and whole life policies may not match those of mutual funds for example, however, the risk of being on a financial roller coaster and losing all of your money, is not as great with these "permanent" types of life insurance policies. In my opinion, a good financial package will consider all of the above, permanent life insurance coupled with wise investment vehicles.

Secret: Another good feature to look for in a term life insurance policy is: Guaranteed Convertibility, this feature will allow you to convert all or a portion of your term policy to universal or whole life policies (the "permanent" policies), which I will discuss next. *Secret*: Some insurance companies may even give you a partial "credit" for the premiums that you paid for the term insurance policy. This credit could be as much as 50% of the premiums paid during the year that you convert your term policy to whole life or universal life insurance.

Guaranteed Convertibility would always work well for people who liked the benefits of a permanent policy such as universal or whole life, however, could only afford term life insurance initially. This feature allowed them the option to "convert" later, at the time of their choice.

Universal life insurance is initially more expensive than term, however, it does not normally increase at scheduled intervals like term and is usually cheaper than whole life when doing an apples-to-apples comparison. Different than whole life, universal life does not normally pay dividends and could have a lower interest rate for cash value accumulation. Universal life insurance offers a policy that can build "cash value" and has the ability for you to pay flexible premiums (higher or lower payments), as the policy grows in regards to its cash value. This means that if you have cash value that has increased in the policy and you choose not to pay your regularly scheduled premium, the regular payment or the difference (of what you should have paid and what was actually paid, for any given month) could be deducted from the cash value. *Secret*: For this reason, I want to stress a very important point: *Enough money has to be paid into this type of policy to keep it in force!* If the interest rate drops and there is not enough cash value in the policy to keep it "funded" (meaning that the insurance company can take payments from the cash value when you don't pay), then you risk having the policy go out-of-force for underpayment. *Secret*: Ask your insurance agent or representative, what's the lowest that the interest rate could ever go and how much of a "Planned Premium" is recommended, should you decide to use this option. A Planned Premium is an amount that is determined by you and your agent, and represents a payment amount that can not only keep your policy in force, but can also build a certain (targeted) amount of cash value. *Secret*: Some companies offer a Planned Premium schedule, which means that if you continue to pay the designated premium as scheduled, then the company will guarantee the policy to be in force for a certain amount of time (in some cases, until you reach age 95 etc.).

Whole Life insurance is the type of policy that offers fixed premiums over the life of the policy, cash value, and dividends payable by the insurance company (although the dividends may not be guaranteed). Whole life insurance is typically more expensive than term or universal Life. *Secret*: If a policy such as this is purchased while the insured is at a young age, the insured can have a relatively low premium to pay and would keep that same premium throughout their lifetime. The whole life policy will typically have a higher interest rate than universal life and thus build up a larger amount of cash value. The cash value in the policy compounds and increases over the years, meaning, you can normally borrow from this type of policy in the form of a loan. *Secret*: This "loan" may have a relatively low interest rate, and should you decide not to pay the loan back (this too is allowed in most cases), then the amount of the loan will normally be deducted from the death benefit or proceeds at the time of your death. Above all, consult your life insurance company for its specific guidelines.

Dividends payable, although not guaranteed, will be distributed to you, the insured, upon the insurance company having made profitable investments. *Secret*: These dividends can quite often be used to: 1. Put back into your policy to reduce the premium payable by you, 2. Put back into the policy to purchase additional insurance, in which case the death benefit would increase, 3. Set aside in a separate interest bearing account at the insurance company, with you, the insured, usually having access to this amount at any time, or 4. Sent to you, the policy owner, in the form of a check.

From my experience, some people think that a decision has to be made to purchase a *single* type of life insurance (i.e. term, whole life etc.), instead of a combination of the two or three types to make up the total amount needed. Let's assume that your insurance professional calculates your individual or family's life insurance requirements using what's called a Needs Evaluation, (a calculation done by an agent or representative to determine what amount of life insurance would be adequate for you and/or your family), and determines that your family needs $500,000 of life insurance. Let's also assume that he quoted you this amount for whole life (which could be more than you'd want to pay), because you really liked all the benefits that came with whole life, and, the agent's evaluation has determined that in the event of a sudden death, $500,000 would be adequate to take care of your family. *Secret:* You could take out a policy for a much smaller amount in whole life and make up the difference with a term life policy, or any combination of term, universal and whole Life. This way, you could still have your whole life policy and your family still gets the $500,000, *providing the term policy does not have a decreasing death benefit.*

Secret: Another benefit of having cash value in your policy is that some policies allow the surrender of or "cashing in" the policy at retirement age, which could allow you to receive the cash value in the form of a monthly check. Since some predict that social security will not be around in the future, this could be one way of supplementing your income at retirement. You could also surrender your policy at any time and receive whatever cash value has accumulated in the policy minus any penalties and/or surrender charges. However, doing so is *not* normally advised, because once you fully surrender or "cash in" a policy, you will no longer have that policy in force for protection if and when it's needed. If you choose to take out a loan or "partial surrender," (meaning not take out all of the available funds), then the policy can most likely continue, however, check with your particular insurance company or agent to determine exactly what effect this will have on the duration of your policy.

In general, individual life insurance policies are based on a person's age, health, whether the person is a smoker or not, and are usually cheaper for females, because statistically, in the past, women have been shown to live longer than men. *Secret*: While life insurance is generally less expensive for women, health insurance on the other hand, tends to be more expensive for women, as women tend to go to the doctor more often than men. Some believe that historically, this is the reason why women have lived longer than men in the past.

As far as discounts are concerned, some insurance companies not only offer discounts for non-smokers, but also offer additional discounts depending on a person's height/weight proportionality, cholesterol and favorable health history.

Secret: When you sign a life insurance application, there is usually a clause that gives the insurance company the right to look into your medical history. This can be done via computer, through the use of the Medical Information Bureau and can reveal to the insurance company any health problems you may currently have or have had in the past. I have sat across a desk from people who I've sold life insurance to, and in some instances, when I would ask if they were ever told they had or were treated for high blood pressure, the answer was often no. However, after the underwriting department checked their medical history, it was often shown that not only was the person aware of his or her high blood pressure, but the data retrieved by the insurance company revealed the actual medication that the person was taking for it.

Although an insurance company can instantly retrieve a lot of information about you, if further information is needed, the company may order records from your personal physician. *Secret*: Some doctor's offices are notoriously slow when sending out a patient's medical records to an insurance company.

Most often, there are only one or two people in these offices, who work one day a week on sending out requested medical records. If you want to help speed up your life insurance application process, call your doctor's office and kindly ask them if they could expedite sending out your medical records to your insurance company when requested to do so. This way, you won't wait in limbo for any (unnecessary) extended length of time.

Secret: When you apply for life insurance and designate the beneficiary to be a minor (son, daughter etc.), the insurance agent or representative should mention that someone be a "custodian" over the death benefit proceeds, should your death occur while the beneficiary is still a minor. This can be done with what is called the: Uniform Transfer To Minors Act or UTMA, and requires the authorization of the insured/policy owner. This concept allows for some degree of accountability with regards to the person in charge of the proceeds (money) paid by the policy. This should help prevent the "custodian" from spending the money on things that have nothing to do with the welfare of the minor involved. Once the minor reaches a recognized legal age for his or her state, the proceeds should then become the property of the minor.

Secret: Another point that I'd like to make reference to, is a term used in the insurance industry called the: Incontestability Period, which means that if an insured's death occurs during (usually), the first two years that a policy is in force, the insurance company has the right to deny paying the death benefit *if they find that the insured lied or misrepresented the truth (at the time of application), and that lie or misrepresentation would have caused the insurance company not to issue the policy in the first place.* I'll state again: Insurance companies can find out things in your medical history from databases such as the Medical Information Bureau or MIB (not to be confused with the infamous men in black), when you apply for a life insurance policy, therefore it pays to be honest.

Secret: If you were to misrepresent your answer to a question on a life insurance application, *the insurance company may not be obligated to tell you the reason you were declined.* This especially holds true if your misrepresentation had to do with the exact medical condition that was the cause of their declining you.

Finally, a company that rates life insurance companies for their strength and stability is Weiss Research. Their web address is: www.weissratings.com. In addition to A.M. Best, Weiss Research is another good source to help you determine the overall strength of an insurance company.

Secret: With some insurance companies, if you were ever diagnosed with a terminal illness such as cancer, and given a specified amount of time to live by your doctor, you may be entitled to the majority of your policy's death benefit (perhaps 75 percent etc.) WHILE YOU'RE STILL LIVING. This is called the Accelerated Death Benefit Rider, and it would be worth it to see if this coverage is included in your policy. *Secret*: Additionally, there is a feature in some life insurance policies called: <u>Waiver of Premium,</u> which means that if you become disabled from your job and you're off from work for 6 months or more (for example), once past 6 months, you may not have to pay for your policy until you go back to work. This is one example; each company has its own stipulations and may drop this coverage in a policy once you have reached a certain age. Lastly, Waiver of Premium coverage should not be confused with <u>Income Disability Insurance,</u> which can pay you a majority of your regular income if you become injured and not able to work. Finally, ask your agent or representative for specifics as they relate to their particular insurance company and whether or not his or her company offers discounts based on you having no health issues, height/weight proportionality, and no family history of certain diseases.

Most reputable insurance companies will offer you such discounts if you qualify for them. As a rule of thumb, many agents don't like to give quotes at preferred rates in the event that you don't qualify for it, leaving them in the awkward position of having to tell you why your rate is now higher than initially quoted. Giving you a higher, non-preferred quote and then telling you later that you qualified for a lower, preferred rate makes life a lot easier for them.

Secret: Generally speaking, you may find that companies that sell primarily life and health insurance only, may have somewhat higher rates for life insurance, than companies that sell multiple product lines such as life, auto, home, health & business insurance. Companies that sell all lines of insurance have more opportunities to make a profit, since they have more of a variety of products to sell and may not have to rely on life insurance exclusively to make a profit and stay in business. *Secret*: Since the companies that sell life & health insurance primarily, rarely sell the other types of insurance, they typically have to pay their agent's a higher commission, which in turn could be passed on to you in the form of higher premiums. Everyone should have some life insurance, and the benefits are endless as to how life insurance can benefit you and your loved ones. Listed below are some of the major benefits:

1. Replace loss of income upon your death
2. Pay off your home/mortgage upon your death
3. Reduce estate taxes payable upon death
4. Help fund a college education
5. Help supplement retirement
6. Provide funds to your church and/or the charitable organization of your choice upon your death.

Buying life insurance is not as straight forward as buying car insurance and your insurance professional should be thorough in explaining the three major types: Term, Universal and Whole life. Just to recap, Term offers death protection with cheaper payments initially, but no cash value accumulation or dividends. Universal life offers cash value accumulation, flexible payment options, with less or more depending on how much cash value has already accumulated in the policy, at which, after a certain point, you could choose not to pay and let the accumulated cash value in the policy pay the premiums. Beware: not paying your premiums could eventually deplete your accumulated funds/cash value, causing your policy to lapse. Lastly, Whole life is usually the most expensive, (initially), of the three and offers guaranteed level payments, dividends (non-guaranteed) and in a lot of cases, the best interest rate.

As you can see, not all life insurance policies offer the same benefit or perform in the same way. *Secret*: If you have a life insurance policy that is canceled for non-payment, you may have to pay a higher monthly premium when and if your policy is reinstated, if your health has changed for the worse during the "out-of-force" period. You may be asked questions regarding changes in your health status and be required to fill out a "reinstatement application." The insurance company will then determine if you are "insurable" as you were originally. This is why it's best to try to keep your life insurance policy from canceling or "lapsing." Additionally, you will have to pay the premiums from the time that your policy "lapsed out," to the current date of the reinstatement. This gap could mean that you have to pay a significant amount to bring the policy back in force and current, especially if your monthly premiums were fairly large.

Secret: Let's assume that you owe a substantial amount to put your life insurance policy back in force, and this amount is more than you are able to pay at the time. You may be able to have the death benefit coverage reduced to a lower amount, in an effort to reduce the amount that you have to pay, to make up for the period that the policy was out of force. With that said, once the policy is back in force, you can perhaps (depending on the company) *at a later date*, decide to increase the death benefit coverage to what it was originally.

This technique was often encouraged by my superiors as a way to help get those life insurance policies "back on the books," and allows you to *affordably* put your life insurance back in force until you can comfortably raise the coverage amount later. Even though you are starting out with less coverage than you had originally, this certainly beats not having any life insurance at all. Note: In the case of universal life insurance, however, this particular technique may not be allowed because of the way that a universal life policy is structured.

As far as billing methods are concerned, most companies (and not just insurance companies) prefer for your payments to be automatically withdrawn from your checking or savings account. Why? They generally prefer this method of payment because studies have shown that you, as a customer, are less likely to "lapse out" or have your insurance canceled as a result of non-payment this way. This could be a possible benefit for both you and the insurance company.

There are a lot of people, however, that do not like having payments automatically withdrawn from their checking or savings accounts. *Secret*: This billing mode seems to be especially annoying at the time that an insurance company has a rate increase (as with car insurance). Some insurance companies may not "effectively" notify their insured(s) when they decide to raise their rates (especially when it comes to car insurance). As a result, you as a customer, may not realize that on the 15th of the month your insurance company will be deducting $140 out of your account instead of the usual $100 payment. Obviously, if you do not have a sufficient amount of money in your account to cover this increase, your account would go into the negative, resulting in bounced checks and horrendous banking fees. In some cases, the insurance company may credit you back for this amount (the fees), provided you show proof of the negative transaction and the bounced check fees that you may have incurred.

I recall times when customers would complain that they were not notified that their insurance rates were going to increase. In my opinion, insurance companies may only passively (if at all) notify consumers for fear that there would be a mass termination of policies (by consumers) to find cheaper auto insurance.

Secret: Another money saving technique concerning life insurance policies is to have a spouse added on to a universal or whole life policy as an "additional insured." One person would be the primary insured on the policy and the other spouse can be "added on" the policy by use of an "additional insured rider, in an effort to make the "total package" more affordable. In most cases, going this route is less expensive than both individuals having their own separate policy, be cause the additional insured's portion of the policy is usually in the form of term insurance, which is cheaper (initially) than both husband and wife having universal or whole life policies.

Secret: I would often talk to a husband and wife about the money-saving benefits of one spouse being added as a rider (i.e. additional insured) to the life insurance policy of the other. However, I would also inform them that whoever is designated to be the primary insured owns the policy, and in the event that the two end up divorcing or separating, the spouse who is the additional insured would still be covered under the policy until the primary insured (or policy owner) decides to exclude or take the other spouse off of the policy. Another important point to know is, even if the couple in this scenario remained happily married, the spouse added on to the policy as an additional insured, would normally see his or her coverage end either at the time of their death, or at a specified age in the policy (age 65 for example), or basically, whichever comes first.

Secret: Finally, life insurance death benefit proceeds can be used as a charitable gift to your favorite organization or church upon your death. For ministers and other heads of religious institutions, a life insurance policy can be set up and paid for by the congregation, so that in the event of the death of the minister or pastor etc., the church can receive the death benefit proceeds. In other words, a minister or priest can make the congregation or parish the beneficiary of his or her life insurance policy. Speaking of beneficiaries, you should also consider naming a "contingent" beneficiary on any life insurance policy that you purchase. The contingent beneficiary could be the next individual in line to receive the death benefit proceeds, should something happen to you and your beneficiary at the same time.

An example of this would be a husband and wife who died in a fatal car accident, they would have been smart to designate a sister, brother or in-law etc. as a contingent beneficiary. The contingent beneficiary could then receive the proceeds in order to take care of the couple's children. If no contingent beneficiary were designated, the proceeds payable would most likely go to the legal guardian of the children or to the insured(s) next of kin. However, I'm sure that most people would like to make this determination themselves, ahead of time, without leaving the responsibility or decision for their state's legal system to decide.

In my experience, I have talked to people who suffered the loss of a family member and had to wait a longer than normal period of time to receive the proceeds from the deceased person's life insurance policy. In all of these cases, the deceased person died within the first two years of their policy being issued. As mentioned earlier in this chapter, this two year Incontestability Period, starting when a life insurance policy is first issued, allows an insurance company to deny a claim, if it discovers that the insured person lied, misrepresented information, or otherwise had a health problem or circumstance that the insurance company did not know of previously, and would have caused the insurance company to not issue the life insurance policy in the first place. Since insurance companies enjoy the possibility of not having to pay under these circumstances, the claims process is thoroughly more "cautious," in an effort to see if something "surfaces," which could allow them the right to deny the claim entirely. *Secret*: As a result, many people have to pay out-of-pocket for their family member's or loved one's funeral expense, and do not receive any death benefit proceeds from the insurance company until after the funeral. Finally, the moral of this story is: Be prepared to pay the funeral cost of your loved one or family member, initially, despite them having life insurance, should their death occur during the first two years of their policy being issued.

CHAPTER 6

10
INSURANCE PRODUCTS
YOU SHOULD KNOW ABOUT!

10 Insurance Products You Should Know Exist!

1. <u>Renter's Insurance</u> is relatively inexpensive and can protect your personal property or "contents," against theft, fire, damage from the elements and just about everything else that a homeowner's insurance policy would cover for personal property. A renter's policy will also include liability coverage (protection for lawsuits), and most insurers offer discounts that can save you quite a bit on your auto insurance if you have renter's insurance with their company.

Secret: Two features that should be included on your renter's policy include: <u>Loss of Use</u> coverage, where the insurance company pays for you and your family to stay in a hotel at the time of a loss, if your primary residence becomes uninhabitable, and until restoration is done. Also, I've found that a lot of people like Loss of Refrigeration coverage. This coverage will pay to replace the food in your refrigerator up to a specified amount, usually $250 to $500, if your food spoiled as the result of a power outage etc. In my experience, customers who reported this type of claim were told to simply make an itemized list of the food products that perished. Additionally, keeping your receipts, videotaping, or photographing your belongings, is especially helpful if you must file a claim regarding your personal property. Insurance companies like for you to fill out itemized reports when you're claiming loss or theft of personal property. Having proof that you actually owned the item(s) is always good, as fraudulent claims have caused most insurance companies to closely scrutinize these situations as they occur. Personal Property Replacement Cost is another "must-have," see the section coming later on Personal Property Replacement Cost for more information.

2. Personal Umbrella is an inexpensive policy that can cover you over and above the liability portion of your homeowner's or auto insurance. Usually, an average homeowner's policy will include $100,000 for liability (auto often less). This extra coverage can be quite useful if you incur a big lawsuit and the damages that you are ordered to pay exceed the limits of your homeowner's or auto insurance policy (whichever line of insurance that applies). Being relatively inexpensive, you may be able to purchase an umbrella policy that will give you an extra $1,000,000 in liability coverage for as little as $200 a year.

3. Long Term Care is an important coverage that will pay for home health care, adult day care and care in an assisted living facility or nursing home, for a specified amount of time or lifetime (depending on the type of plan purchased). Not to be confused with health insurance, Long Term Care describes any type of extended maintenance or personal care services you may need when you are not able to take care of yourself due to illness, injury or a cognitive disability such as Alzheimer's disease. More importantly, like life insurance, this coverage needs to be purchased before you actually need to use it. It's a good idea to buy this insurance while you're still "eligible" health wise. *Secret*: Many people don't realize until it's too late, that Medicare does not cover most Long Term

Care. Medicare only covers care by a licensed professional that is needed every day of the week for patients who are *getting better*. The same also holds true for most private health insurance plans. Medicaid, on the other hand, will pay for Long Term Care, *but only after all of your resources have been depleted.* Therefore, Long Term Care Insurance should be considered to help during the "Golden Years" and help lessen the financial burden on family and/or loved ones.

4. <u>Personal Property Replacement Cost</u> is a coverage that can usually be added to your renter's or homeowner's policy for a nominal amount, usually between $30 and $60 per year. With this coverage, your personal property would be valued at current market value (as in brand new) instead of a depreciated value (think used), if it had to be replaced. This coverage is not normally included in a policy, due to the fact that the intent of insurance is to replace a covered item with another of similar value and condition, or repair a damaged item to its original condition. However, this coverage is certainly worth purchasing, considering how relatively inexpensive it can be.

Secret: As mentioned previously, most companies will offer the full replacement if you have this coverage and *actually replace* the covered items. However, should you decide to keep the money that the insurance company is offering for settlement (without replacing the items), then they will normally pay you based on an actual cash value (depreciated basis or used) and not full replacement.

Secret: Most insurance companies will pay you an amount equal to the actual cash value first, and look to pay you the *difference* for full replacement, once you have documented proof that you've actually replaced the covered item(s).

5. <u>Leased Gap Insurance</u> will pay the difference between what you owe on your leased vehicle and what your vehicle is actually worth at the time of a loss. Many consumers become "upside down" with their auto financing, meaning that they owe

more on their vehicle than it is worth at the time of a total loss. Leased Gap insurance will pay for the difference in these two amounts. This coverage was previously offered by car dealerships and is now being offered by many auto insurers.

Additionally, Loan Gap Insurance can accomplish the same for those who have financed their vehicles. *Secret*: This coverage may be cheaper to get from an insurance company than a car dealer, because you are not paying interest on this coverage with a normal auto insurance policy, since it is not part of a finance contract.

6. Uninsured Motorist Property Damage (U.M.P.D.) this (quietly inexpensive), coverage should be offered when someone purchases automobile liability insurance only. This coverage will pay to fix your car if someone hits your vehicle in a collision, and the at-fault person does not have any auto liability insurance. Most often, you will be required to get the at-fault driver's personal information (name, address, DL# etc.) Therefore, U.M.P.D. will not normally apply in a hit and run incident, when the at-fault driver's information is not known. There is usually a limit ($15,000 for example), as to how much will be paid under this endorsement. However, this limit is normally sufficient to cover damages for many older vehicles that were covered with liability only.

7. Communication Device Coverage is useful in this day and age of cell phones, pagers and a host of other technological gadgets. This coverage can pay for communication equipment stolen or damaged in your vehicle. Coverage basically applies to equipment that did not actually come with the vehicle, but was included later as an upgrade, purchased separately, or included by the vehicle's manufacturer on more expensive vehicles. *Secret*: This coverage can also compensate you if part of your claim included the theft or destruction of your communication device.

8. <u>Home Day Care Endorsement</u> is a "must-have" coverage for home child care providers and can usually be added to a homeowner's or renter's policy for those who operate a child day care service from home. This coverage will provide extra liability to protect the homeowner/day care operator in case of a lawsuit, pertaining to children who were in the home-owner's or daycare operator's care at the time of an "incident," involving a child or children. *Secret*: Check with your insurance company to see if they have a limit on the amount of children that can be covered under this endorsement at any one time. An average maximum amount of children usually covered under this endorsement is six.

9. <u>10-20 Pay Whole Life Policies</u> are whole life policies that can be "paid in full" in just 10 or 20 years, while offering death protection and cash value accumulation in the policy for the duration of an insured person's lifetime, or until the end of the policy (whichever occurs first). With these types of policies, there are no more payments after 10 or 20 years, compared to a "normal" whole life policy that is payable until age 95, 100, or the death of the insured, whichever comes first.

This type of policy was always a favorite among parents and grand parents as "gifts" for their children or grand children. For a young person, this policy is relatively inexpensive and in my experience, was attractive and more of a big seller to younger people.

Secret: The nice thing about these types of policies is that the cash value can continue to build even after the policy is "paid for" in 10 to 20 years. This normally tax-deferred money can be used in several ways, including "borrowing" against your policy in the form of a loan. What you may not know is, you may not have to pay the amount back that you borrowed. However, at the time of your death, any outstanding "loan" amount will be deducted from the death benefit proceeds payable from the policy.

10. <u>Buy-Sell Agreement</u> is beneficial for partners in business. This "life insurance" coverage pays for the "buy out" of one of the partners in a partnership with the proceeds going to the deceased partner's spouse or next of kin. This is done so that the remaining partner can "buy the other partner out" to retain a total ownership of the business. *Secret*: If this coverage is to be considered, an attorney should be consulted to help determine specific details, in the event of the death of one of the partners or owners.

CHAPTER 7

INSURANCE BUYING TIPS
FOR THE NEW MILLENIUM

Today, plenty of people are buying insurance products over the Internet. Some say that they are saving money because the competing insurance companies online often offer insurance through different carriers, generally have less overhead and the buying process appears to be quicker and more streamlined, which can make for a more convenient process.

However, I also want to point out the added value that a good, professional insurance agent can provide. Major insurance companies are finding out every day that people like buying insurance through agents: most people are interested in building a relationship with their agent in order to *get more accountability* for their hard-earned money, *and to have a professional advise them* (one on one) regarding their need for insurance. The challenge here is to find a good agent & company.

These days, many large insurance companies not only have a presence on the Internet, but are also combining this presence with their "agent force" to have what they feel will be a winning combination. Many see this arrangement as having the best of both worlds. Consumers will ultimately be able to manage their accounts online and make immediate changes to some of their coverage(s) when necessary. You will want to keep this in mind when considering your next insurance purchase. Listed below is a checklist of tips that I have known to be helpful to many of my clients in the past:

1. It's a good idea to have your insurance agent do what's called a "Personal Insurance Evaluation," which will uncover any "gaps" to see if you are under insured in certain areas or perhaps over insured (which can perhaps save you some money), this "evaluation" can pertain to all lines of insurance.

2. When buying life insurance, make sure your agent does what's called a "Life Insurance Needs Evaluation," which is a more accurate way of determining how much *life insurance* you and your family need for financial protection.

3. To help reduce the theft of some of the more frequently stolen cars, some insurance companies have offered <u>Vehicle Glass Etching</u>, which encompasses engraving your vehicles identification number into the vehicle's glass. The idea here is to discourage car thieves by making the car's parts more traceable if stolen. Interestingly enough, some insurers have offered this service for free to their insured(s).

4. If you have a home or auto claim less than $2,000 to $2,500 for example, your insurance company may be able to settle your claim faster with what is called a "fast pay" or "quick payout," which means that your agent may be able to write you a check without you having to go through the usual process, which takes longer to get your claim settled.

It is also advised that you do not make statements regarding your possible responsibility (for being at-fault) for an accident etc., until you have been advised as such by your insurance company. Remember, determination of liability is a matter of law and not of opinion.

5. When you already have existing full-coverage or liability insurance with an insurance company, most reputable compa-

nies allow you to extend that same coverage to a newly purchased vehicle for a period of (usually) thirty days from the date of purchase. This way, you have some time before you have to initiate a down payment, to start a policy for the newly purchased vehicle. *Secret*: If you only had liability on the existing vehicle, then only liability would extend to your newly purchased vehicle and the same holds true for full-coverage. This allows you time to contact your insurance company to have the new vehicle added to your policy. Note: When referring to new in this case, it means newly purchased by you, the vehicle can actually be new or used.

6. Many people are not aware that if you hit a pothole and sustain damage to your vehicle, your insurance company (under Collision coverage) may cover this damage.

7. In most instances, rental reimbursement coverage can only be added to your auto insurance policy when you have full coverage insurance and *not* when you only have liability coverage. A rental is usually authorized in conjunction with an insurance claim and not for use when a policyholder's vehicle is being repaired (from normal wear & tear) or when a rental vehicle is needed, as in the case of a road trip.

8. If you will be married or a year older within 60-90 days for example, and being married or a year older will reduce your auto insurance rate, be sure to tell your insurance company. Some companies will allow your rate to be based on that particular age or marital status, given that the change of status will be occurring soon.

9. If an accident is *not* believed to be your fault and the responsible driver either has no insurance or is with a "substandard" insurance company, you may want to consider having your insurance company fix your car, if your insurer is reputable and has good claims service. In my experience, dealing with a substandard company has been a nightmare for a lot of people. Either they had to go through a lot of red tape, had to

have their car repaired at shady repair shops and/or had to wait an unusually extended length of time to get their vehicle repaired. This is why, even though an accident may not be your fault, you can consider having your insurance company fix your vehicle, if you encounter "problems" when dealing with the other driver's insurance company. In this case, you will have to pay your deductible and you will most likely have a "non-chargeable" claim on your driving record. Your insurance company would normally attempt to recover the cost to repair your vehicle *and* your deductible from the at-fault driver's insurance company (if any). If the at-fault driver is with a reputable company with good claims service, it is highly recommended that you put in your claim through *their* insurance company. To do this, you would call the other driver's agent directly or get the number needed (from the other company's home office) to report claims. This way, you avoid having a claim put on your driving record (when not at-fault) and you should not have to pay a deductible amount. This is normally advised when an accident is not your fault and the other driver is with a good insurance company.

A word of caution: In certain states there have been reports of street gangs staging auto accidents in an effort to collect money for supposed injuries.

10. If your vehicle has any expensive third party or "aftermarket" parts, such as high-end audio, expensive rims, custom bodywork etc., let your insurance company know so they can make allowance for this extra equipment and cover it. The reason I say this is because insurance companies will (generally) only cover a vehicle with standard equipment installed from the manufacturer, unless they are previously informed otherwise.

11. Always check the Vehicle Identification Number or V.I.N. on your application and proof of insurance cards for accuracy.

You would be surprised as to how often insurance companies and agents record numbers and/or alphabet letters in the V.I.N. inaccurately. Many times, drivers are hassled by the police (when stopped) because of these inaccuracies.

12. Be sure to get a receipt for any payments made (especially cash). Some insurance companies have an internal problem when it comes to employee dishonesty. Some insurance agents don't accept cash payments either (for security reasons).

13. Be sure to inquire about an "accident free" discount for being accident free with an insurance company, find out if and when you would be entitled to this discount, if offered by your insurer.

14. If you get a cancellation letter from an insurance company indicating that your insurance will cancel on June 15th for example, in most cases, what they are really telling you is that your insurance will cancel at 12:01 a.m. the night of June 14th, which is technically June 15th. However, a lot of people will still rush into an agent's office to deliver their payment on the 15th. This can result in a "break" in coverage and depending on the insurance company, you could be charged a higher premium once your policy has lapsed. Not to mention, if you suffered some type of "loss" during this "break" in coverage.

15. Most larger, reputable insurance companies will either not offer you auto insurance or will charge you a much higher rate if you did not have 6 months of prior, continuous (at least liability) coverage. To get around this, a lot of people will get insurance through a substandard insurance company for 6 months and then "switch" to a preferred carrier at the completion of the 6-month term.

16. *Secret*: If you decide to pay the higher rate (in the above scenario), you will normally have that higher rate for 6 consecutive months and may have to notify your agent or company when the 6 month period is up. Furthermore, if you only

had 3 months of prior insurance, these 3 prior months combined with 3 additional months from your new insurer, should satisfy your 6 month (total) requirement and enable you to qualify for their preferred rate, providing that all other things (i.e.; your driving record and claims history etc.) remain acceptable.

17. If you get a ticket for a moving violation and your state has a Traffic Safety School program, and you attend the designated "class" on driving safety etc., then your speeding ticket (or moving violation), should not go on your driving record, as reported to insurance companies. It is highly recommended that you consider this option. It may cost you a little more to attend this "school." However, the amount of money that you can save by not having 1 or 2 tickets on your driving record can make a HUGE difference in your insurance premiums.

18. *Secret*: Carefully check over your insurance application(s) for any questions answered, that were not asked of you. Many times, some insurance agents (in a hurry), will answer certain questions on your behalf, making their own assumptions. This could cause you frustration later, once you've signed the application, so be sure to recheck those answers!

More Points To Consider

Many reputable insurance companies will not use third party or "aftermarket" parts on your vehicle if your vehicle is less than 2-3 years old. It is a good idea to ask your insurance company what their policy is involving aftermarket parts. Aftermarket parts are parts replaced on vehicles that were manufactured by companies other than the vehicle's original manufacturer. Ask your insurance company's claim representative if the insurance company and body repair shop offer a guarantee for the aftermarket parts used, as well as for their workmanship. *Secret*: An aftermarket part should be identified as such on your repair estimate and may be identified as a "quality replacement part." For safety reasons, aftermarket parts are frequently *not* used to replace equipment that protects occupants in a vehicle during an accident. This refers to items such as airbags, seat belts, bumper reinforcement, installation parts and impact bars.

Secret: There have also been reports of car mechanics stealing expensive airbags out of cars in their possession and replacing the airbags with things such as dirty towels and even paper trash. Sadly, these airbags are then sold for profit without regard to the concern or safety of the vehicle's owner and occupants.

Secret: Some reputable companies will still use original car manufacturer's equipment (also called OEM parts) at the vehicle owner's insistence. However, you as the vehicle owner may be required to pay the difference between the price of the aftermarket part and the price of the original manufacturer's part. Finally, insurance companies state: That by using aftermarket parts responsibly, they can pass on the savings to their customers in the form of affordable insurance rates. Check with your state regarding the use of aftermarket parts, as each state's position on the use of such parts can differ greatly.

Buying life and health insurance through group plans is generally less expensive because the group (as a whole) is sharing in the cost of the total premium for the insurance. However, keep these important points in mind when buying life insurance through a group plan:

1. Once you leave your group/employer, you may not be entitled to your life or health insurance any longer, be sure to ask about the consequences of severing ties from your employer, ahead of time.

2. The amount of insurance coverage available for you as an employee or group member is usually limited to a certain type and amount.

3.) Group/employer supplied life insurance is usually term insurance and does not offer any opportunity to build cash value. As mentioned previously, accumulated cash value can help supplement your retirement, help pay for a child's college education and provide an emergency resource of funds if needed.

Some popular products include Variable life insurance policies. These policies offer death benefit protection and allocate a certain percentage of the premiums paid toward investment vehicles such as mutual funds. Most large insurance companies have sophisticated software that can help analyze what you and your family's financial needs may be and which of their products might be a proper fit for your situation.

I want to mention a very important point: *Buy life insurance with the intent on keeping it*. A lot of people pay for their life insurance policy and then let it lapse, resulting in money thrown away and the risk of dying unexpectedly without having any life insurance at all. I personally know of several cases where people thought enough to buy life insurance to protect their families in the event that something happened to them. However, in one particular case, the policy eventually lapsed and during the lapsed period, this one individual had a heart attack. Fortunately, he survived the heart attack, however, he had to re-apply for his life insurance *and* run the risk of either paying a "new" higher premium (due to his "new" health condition) or worse, no longer being insurable by most insurance companies.

Insurance companies will often decline people who have had serious heart and health ailments such as strokes, heart attacks, cancer and the list goes on and on. *Secret*: If you or someone you know is having difficulty getting life insurance through normal channels, search for a type of company that specializes in what is called "impaired risk" coverage. These are insurance companies that will insure people with health conditions that most insurance companies will not insure. I have seen one particular company's claim (in an advertisement) that they will insure people that are HIV positive, depending on the severity or state of the condition.

Sadly, I have also witnessed cases where a young person whom had life insurance was killed and the insurance company involved, denied (paying out) the claim because the person was reportedly killed during illegal activity *and* had a prior criminal history, which the insurance company did not know about initially. An insurance company could deny a claim if an answer to a question (such as: Have you ever been convicted of a felony?) was misrepresented, especially if the death of the insured occurred during the Incontestability Period (the first two years of the policy, for example). It's best to be honest during the life insurance application process. As stated earlier, insurance companies have the resources to find out about your medical, and even financial background.

Most people familiar with life insurance know that a smoker will pay more for the same type and amount of life insurance than a non-smoker. *Secret*: What you may not know is that some companies will regard a cigar/pipe smoker and tobacco chewer as *non-smokers*.

As mentioned previously, you may find rates for life insurance lower with insurance companies that sell multi-line insurance products such as auto, home, business, health and life, as opposed to a company that just sells life insurance almost exclusively. Additionally, look for a life or health insurance policy that allows for a "free look period." This "period," which is usually limited to 10 or 30 days, begins after you have received your policy, and allows you to return it to the insurance company for cancellation and a full refund of premium, if you are not completely satisfied with it.

As the process of getting life insurance policies approved and "issued" has traditionally been slow, new technology is enabling insurance companies to complete the whole process (in some cases without the application ever touching human hands), by scanning your signature while you are sitting in the agent's office and submitting the application (to the home office) over the company's computer network.

CHAPTER 8

THE INSIDER-SECRETS TO SAVING MONEY ON AUTO INSURANCE

This section will focus on some of the "inside" tricks for saving money on your auto insurance. The first thing that I want to mention is that when you decide to change insurance companies, once you are accepted and approved by your new insurer, call your previous insurer and make sure that they cancel your auto insurance promptly.

A lot of people think that their new insurance company will do this for them or that their insurance will just lapse or "run out." The reason that I mention this is because your prior insurance carrier may continue to keep you covered for an additional 30 days or so, not knowing that you've purchased insurance elsewhere.

As a result, your prior insurance company is going to look for you to pay for this period of coverage (referred to as earned premium) and will not hesitate to refer your account to a collection agency if not paid. In most cases, if you show your prior insurer proof that you have insurance elsewhere, they will usually waive the premium that they are seeking for this period of time.

Now let's talk a little about youthful drivers. Most reputable insurance companies want all of the drivers in your household listed on an insurance policy (whether any youthful drivers drive a particular insured vehicle or not). Even if you told most companies that your youthful driver does not drive your car, your insurance company will still expect you to pay higher rates and include the younger driver on your policy.

Assuming that the youthful driver is under the age of 25, you may be able to sign what's called a <u>Named Driver Exclusion</u> form, which means that (you agree that) the younger driver will *not* be covered if he operates your insured vehicle(s). However, this also means that you are not paying a higher premium because of the youthful driver. Being excluded should not matter as much if the youthful driver never actually drives the vehicle in the first place.

Another money saver is to inquire if you can get a <u>Good Student Discount</u>. This will save you money and usually requires that the youthful driver is under age 25, *and* has at least a "B" grade average (which may have to be verified by having a form signed by a school official). *Secret*: The Good Student Discount normally has a bigger (money-saving) impact for male drivers, while female drivers usually fare better with the discount given for having your homeowner's and car insurance with the same company.

One of the surprising "secrets" that you may not know when it comes to insuring young drivers is: As mentioned earlier, insurance companies want the young driver in the household listed on your auto insurance policy. If it's one vehicle, for example (belonging to the parents and there's more drivers than cars), then the young driver will most likely be listed as an *occasional driver*. An auto policy is normally "rated" (meaning the price that you have to pay) according to the youngest driver in the household. *Secret*: To save money, the idea is to have the younger driver rated on either the oldest vehicle in the household, or better yet, one that has liability coverage only. *With most good insurance companies, the young driver will be covered no matter which car he or she drives. So, why not list him or her on the vehicle which will be the* **least** *expensive to insure,* since the insurance company requires the young driver in the household to be listed as a driver on *at least one vehicle*. This technique of course would not apply in the above example of the Named Driver Exclusion, which would mean that the young driver would not be covered on the vehicle in question.

Students who attend college away from home for the majority of the year should be able to list the car that he or she drives primarily, as being "garaged" at the school address. Basically, this means that for most of the year, this is where the car will be kept and the rate for this vehicle should be charged accordingly. If you are the parent of a student and you pay for the insurance, you should be able to have your insurance company send the bill to you while having the vehicle's "rate" being based at the college address. This may save you quite a bit of money, especially if the college is in a small rural town and you live in a big city.

For older drivers, some states offer a defensive driving course for people over the age of 55. Upon completing the course, you should be given proof of completion to show your insurance company, which may in turn, offer discounts for successfully completing the course.

Another money saver is to have your insurance premiums deducted from your checking account each month (if you pay on a monthly basis), this could not only save you money in monthly service charges, but will also save you postage and any potential late fees that you may incur as a result of delayed mail etc.

Additionally, if you have 3 cars insured by one insurance company and each car is on a separate account, you are most likely paying three separate service fees, when you could combine all the cars on to one account and pay just one monthly fee. Combining all three vehicles on to one account can also help you to manage your payments better, since all three vehicles will most likely have the same due date.

CHAPTER 9

INSURANCE &
THE SERIOUS THREAT
OF TERRORISM

I want to start by reiterating the same message that the American media has been conveying to the general public since the events of September 11, 2001: America and its concern for security has changed forever. Insurance has certainly been of more interest since September 11 and with that said, I wish to shed some light on this matter as it applies to such terrible events.

Some insurance companies that are considered stock companies are more likely to be affected financially by what has occurred, as investors react to the ramifications that the terrorist attacks and financial scandals have had on the U.S. economy.

However, all insurance companies are not owned by stockholders. Some are considered to be mutual companies and are "owned" by their policyholders. Some of the biggest names fall into either one of these two categories. Overall, there appears to be some questions and concerns as to how insurance claims are settled (if at all) for individuals and families affected by terrorism. Here are some general points to consider, but by no means, hard and fast rules:

1. Some insurance company policies state that the company will provide coverage for auto and homeowner claims, as a result of terrorism, while excluding (or not providing), coverage for "acts of war," either declared or undeclared.

2. Some companies have life insurance policies that *do not* exclude coverage for terrorist acts, however, *do* exclude optional coverage(s) such as Waiver of Premium and the Accidental Death Benefit Rider, if needed as a result of direct or indirect war or service in the military. **Waiver of Premium** calls for the insurance company to "waive" premiums for a life insurance policy (usually after a specified "waiting period") should the covered person become disabled and not able to work. The **Accidental Death Benefit Rider** calls for the insurance company to pay an extra, pre-determined amount specified by a life insurance policy, should the covered person's death be ruled accidental. Both of these coverage(s) are normally optional and should be requested if desired. I have believed for a long time that one should not rely on a life insurance policy containing Accidental Death Benefit coverage alone.

3. Business or Commercial insurance policies may not exclude acts of terrorism in general, but *may exclude* coverage for Loss of Income and/or Business Interruption as a result of an act of terrorism. However, these things are usually *not excluded* if the business sustains an *accidental, covered physical loss.*

If America is ever at war with another country and that war carries over to U.S. soil, damages to the property of Americans may not be covered. Additionally, some travel insurance policies may contain language that excludes acts of terrorism. Furthermore, people in our military may see similar exclusions and could end up "uncovered" due to an "act of war" exclusion that could be implemented (in the future), into policies written for them.

<u>The bottom line is this</u>: In the past, insurance policies have not necessarily been written to contemplate the type of event we have seen on September 11, 2001 and insurance companies may very well change the way that policies are written, as well as the language that such policies contain.

CHAPTER 10

BASICS FOR PROTECTING YOUR BUSINESS

Some of the more popular business insurance policies are called BOP policies (meaning Business Owner's Package) and come in various forms. You will want to be clear on what "level" or form of coverage you purchase, if you are a business owner. The BOP policy could come in a "Basic Form" which may cover fire, smoke, wind and hail damage, lightning, aircraft and vehicle collision, vandalism, riot and sprinkler leakage. There could be an option for "Broad Form" coverage, which may include everything in the Basic Form coverage *plus* damage from the weight of snow and ice, falling objects, glass breakage and water damage from interior frozen & cracked pipes. Lastly, the most inclusive option could be what's called "Special Form" coverage, which could include all covered losses under the Broad coverage *plus* other types of direct physical losses that are not limited or excluded in the policy.

Secret: If you are a landlord, your property may qualify for a BOP policy, and a good policy will provide for you to continue to receive your rental income, should your tenants be forced to leave due to a covered loss. A good policy will also provide replacement cost coverage (where the insurance company does not deduct for depreciation) for your business personal property. Your business personal property can include appliances and fixtures etc., which are for tenant use, and, which are not considered a part of the actual building. Basically, this property belongs to you as a landlord, and in the case of a storeowner, in-stock merchandise would fall under this category. A perfect example of business personal property would be a washer and dryer that you own, which are for tenant use, and on the premises of your rental property.

Another important consideration when buying business insurance is the liability factor, as a landlord, you'll want to have higher than normal limits of liability, at least $500,000 per occurrence and $1,000,000 total for any given year. More importantly, with the relatively inexpensive cost of liability coverage, it is recommended that you consider limits even higher, such as $1,000,000 per occurrence and $2,000,000 total for any given policy year.

Secret: When you insure more than one rental property with a particular insurance company (for example 4 or 5+ properties), ask your agent if you are eligible for a multi-property discount. Since I was in the business of selling insurance, I knew that such a discount was available and would make it known to my clients, however, I do know of a great deal of agent's who did not offer this discount, *unless* they were in a strong competitive bid to earn someone's business.

Secret: In addition, insurance companies can often allow discounts in the form of "credits" to businesses and owners of rental properties (apt. & office buildings) for such things as: having managerial experience, whether or not the property has a sprinkler system, non-combustible/fire resistive construction, and/or a smoke & fire alarm detection system, to name a few. *Secret*: It's worth repeating: Insurance companies may offer these types of discounts when they are in competition for your business, however, these discounts may not necessarily be "volunteered" to you, so, now that you know they exist, be sure to ask!

Secret: I know of cases where a person owned 2 or 3 rental properties listed together on one policy and notified their agent that they had recently sold *one* of their properties, and to have the policy cancelled, since insurance was no longer needed *for that particular property*. The agent then notified his or her home office to cancel the policy, not realizing at the time that the policy covered 2 or 3 different properties. As a result, **all of the insurance on all of the properties was cancelled**. Fortunately, the insurance company was reputable and fair, they acknowledged their agent's or representative's mistake and reinstated the remaining policies (which should not have been cancelled), *back to the effective date of the cancellation*.

If you're a business owner, (like most other business owners) you run the risk of potentially getting sued and having to pay a huge lawsuit or settlement, should you be found liable to others in some way. *Secret*: Even if your regular business insurance policy offers liability protection, it is definitely worth purchasing a Commercial Blanket Liability policy, which can protect you over and above what your regular business policy will cover. For example, suppose you owned a restaurant and one of your employees (waiter or waitress) accidentally spilled hot coffee on one of your patrons, more than likely, your patron is going to sue your business for damages. Perhaps your business policy contained $500,000 worth of liability coverage, however, the legal settlement (including attorney's fees) that you were ordered to pay totaled $875,000. Would you have an extra $375,000 on hand to pay the difference?

Most small business owners don't have this kind of money and one lawsuit like this could potentially put most people out of business. The good news is that for approximately $200 to

$300 a year, you could purchase a Blanket Excess Liability policy, which could (depending on the amount chosen), have easily handled the $375,000 that would have been needed in the above example. The problem with a lot of insurance situations is that this type of (Blanket Excess Liability) policy may not have been offered to you and you would not have known to ask for it, if you did not know that such a policy exists. A good insurance agent or representative will recognize this need and should offer you this type of coverage, however, this is not always the case.

Secret: Many insurance companies have custom designed "packages" for common businesses, such as a contractor's package, a body/repair shop package, a religious institution package and so on. These "packages" will have coverage(s) specifically geared towards the particular business for which each was designed.

Secret: I cannot stress enough, the importance of purchasing additional liability insurance for your business, which is essentially for protection. If you look at the amount of extra coverage that you can get for a relatively small amount of extra premium, you will see that the liability portion of your policy is not expensive at all. As mentioned earlier in this section, there are specific "packages" that insurance companies develop, that are made for common types of businesses, and there are other types of "packages" that contain the most needed basics, however, allow the business owner to add additional, optional coverage(s) as needed, on an "a'la carte" basis.

These "add-ons" could be anything from coverage for employee dishonesty (you can file a claim if one of your employee's steals money from the business, usually with a maximum coverage limit of $10,000 or more), loss of refrigeration (if the power goes out in a restaurant for example, spoiling the establishment's inventory), coverage for valuable papers, computer fraud, money orders and counterfeit paper currency, to name a few.

Professional Liability insurance is the type of liability that will offer protection for professionals, should they become the target of a lawsuit arising out of performing the duties of their profession. When most people think of this type of insurance, they think of only Doctors, Dentists and the threat of malpractice suits. However, there is also professional liability for Barbers, Beauticians and Clergy etc. Professional Liability Insurance (also known as Errors & Omissions or E&O), can cover many other professions as well, including: Accountants, Mortgage Brokers, Investment Advisors and Real Estate Agents, Brokers, and Appraisers, Abstractors and Title Agents, Escrow Agents, Attorneys, Engineers and Architects, the Media, Consultants, Information Technology Professionals and Directors & Officer's coverage for both profit and non-profit companies. Some industries *require* Professional Liability insurance; others don't have a mandatory requirement for it. It will normally be up to you, the business owner, to make sure that you and your employees are adequately covered.

Secret: Policies that are available which you may not know about include: <u>Buy-Sell Agreement</u>, which is a type of policy that is beneficial in a partnership, where if one covered partner dies during the partnership, then the surviving partner will receive death benefit proceeds to "buy the other partner out" or buy out the other partner's share of ownership (in other words, pay the deceased partner's heirs for their share of ownership). Another policy called: <u>Key Person Insurance,</u> can pay you as the business owner for losses sustained to your business, as the result of the death of the "key person," who was largely responsible for the success of the business.

Most states may require you as an employer to have workmen's compensation coverage, which will pay a certain percentage of your employee's salary if the employee is injured on the job. *Secret*: You as the owner of the business should have the *option* to include this coverage for yourself, and workmen's compensation may not be required for the owner. Whether or not you as an owner should be included in workmen's compensation coverage, could depend on, if you're involved in performing the actual work, which could result in some type of work related injury. Workmen's compensation can be very costly, some insurance companies will give you a lower rate if you already have other business insurance policies with the company. *Secret*: If your business is caught without workmen's compensation insurance for your employees, you could be faced with huge daily fines for each day that your employees were not covered.

Some insurance companies are more conservative than others and will only insure certain types of businesses that they perceive as less of a risk. Therefore, if you are told that your type of business does not qualify within the guidelines of a particular company, see if the agent or company can refer you to a company that will insure your type of business. Many times, larger insurance companies will have other companies that they "broker out" to, for the types of insurance that they do not offer. *Secret*: Be persistent when seeking help in this area, as some agents may not feel that it's worth the trouble for them to obtain this type of coverage for you, as the process is usually more involved. I have seen some agents avoid these types of cases, when the commission they would receive was (according to them) not worth the effort.

CHAPTER 11

CYBER-RISK:
THE LURKING
INTERNET THREAT

A relatively new type of important insurance protection is called <u>CyberRisk</u> coverage. As Internet security is now more of a prevalent concern, companies are now able to purchase CyberRisk protection, to provide for their liability due to unauthorized access to their computer network and/or system, and to provide coverage for damage to their system as a result of such unauthorized access. As of the writing of this book, a recent news story involved hackers gaining access to the USA Today newspaper's web site, and replacing the company's content with their own.

The Internet has evolved at such a rapid pace, that many insurance companies are now forced to keep up with the technological trends and needs of businesses online. *Secret*: In most cases, a business's general liability policy will not be adequate and is not designed to protect the business in Cyberspace. An adequate CyberRisk (or Ecommerce Insurance) policy can protect your business against the following:

1. Computer virus attacks which impair your business
2. Malicious acts committed by your employees or those

outside of your company's computer network
3. Extortion
4. Destruction of data and records
5. Stolen proprietary information (intellectual property) and trade secrets
6. Damage to a third party's computer network
7. Disruption of your business's computer system or network resulting in "down time"

Secret: When your business is on the Internet, your exposure is worldwide and you're going to need insurance that protects you on a *global basis*. Most traditional insurance policies are limited to the territories and possessions of the United States only.

Lastly, with so much to lose (including damage done by hackers), business owners at risk should definitely consider installing firewalls, implementing internal security measures, procedures for personnel to abide by and last but not least, purchasing E-commerce insurance. Going into greater detail about CyberRisk coverage is beyond the scope of this book. However, it is imperative to let you know that such coverage exists, and more information is available online, including the specific companies that offer it.

Some Final Thoughts

Insurance doesn't have to be complicated, mysterious or even frustrating. A strong, reputable insurance company, with knowledgeable and friendly agents can make a world of difference, before and more importantly, at a "time of loss."

However, consumers as a whole, should know the basics about insurance, as well as be privy to some of the "inside" tips and tricks that can make a difference *and* save them money.

Within the preceding pages of this book, I have tried to share some of both. The following pages contain some important telephone numbers, as well as website addresses for State Insurance and Motor Vehicle Departments, which I hope you will find helpful.

Lastly, I wish you and your family good health, prosperity and longevity. Rejoice in all of the good things that life has to offer!

All the best,
Rodger Nelson

Appendix

Helpful Resources

State Insurance Department Telephone Numbers

State Motor Vehicle Departments

Insurance Glossary

State Insurance Department Telephone Numbers

AZ: (602) 912-8400	**CA**: (916) 445-5544	**CO**: (303) 894-7499
CT: (203) 297-3800	**DC**: (202) 727-8002	**DE**: (302) 739-4251
FL: (904) 922-3100	**GA**: (404) 656-2056	**GU**: (671) 477-5144
HI: (808) 586-2790	**IA**: (515) 281-5705	**ID**: (208) 334-2250
IL: (217) 782-4515	**KS**: (913) 296-7801	**KY**: (502) 564-3630
LA: (504) 342-5900	**MA**: (617) 727-3357	**MD**: (410) 333-6200
ME: (207) 582-8707	**MI**: (517) 373-9273	**MN**: (612) 296-6848
MO: (314) 751-2640	**MS**: (601) 359-3569	**MT**: (406) 444-2040
NC: (919) 733-7349	**ND**: (701) 224-2440	**NH**: (603) 271-2261
NJ: (609) 292-5363	**NM**: (505) 827-4500	**NV**: (702) 687-4270
NY: (212) 602-0203	**OK**: (405) 521-0071	**OR**: (503) 378-4271
PA: (717) 787-5173	**PR**: (809) 722-8686	**RI**: (401) 277-2223
SC: (803) 737-6160	**SD**: (605) 773-3563	**TN**: (615) 741-2241
TX: (512) 463-6464	**UT**: (801) 538-3800	**VA**: (804) 371-97411
VI: (809) 774-2991	**VT**: (802) 828-3301	**WA**: (206) 753-7301
WI: (608) 266-0102	**WV**: (304) 558-3394	**WY**: (307) 777-7401

National Insurance Consumer Helpline (NICH)

1(800) 942-4242

State Motor Vehicle Departments

Alabama

Alabama Department of Public Safety, Driver's Licenses
P.O. Box 1471 Montgomery, Alabama 36102-1471
Telephone: (334) 242-4400
www.dps.state.al.us/

Alaska

State of Alaska, Division of Motor Vehicles
Attn: Driving Records
2760 Sherwood Lane, Suite B
Juneau, Alaska 99801
Telephone (907) 269-5551
www.state.ak.us/dmv/

Arizona

Arizona Department of Transportation
Motor Vehicle Division
P.O. Box 2100
Phoenix, AZ 85001-2100
Telephone: Phoenix - (602) 255-0072,
Tucson - (520) 629-9808
Elsewhere in Arizona (800) 251-5866
www.dot.state.az.us/MVD/mvd.htm

Arkansas

Arkansas Dept. of Motor Vehicles,
Attn: Driving Records,
Room 1130 P.O. Box 1272
Little Rock, Arkansas 72203
Telephone: (501) 682-7052
www.state.ar.us/dfa/odd/motor_vehicle.html

California
Department of Motor Vehicles, Office of Information Services
Public Operations Unit G199
P.O. Box 944247
Sacramento, CA 94244-2470
Telephone (800) 777-0133 or (916) 657-7669 for
out of state calls
www.dmv.ca.gov/

Colorado

Colorado Department of Revenue, Motor Vehicle
Division,
1881 Pierce St.
Lakewood, CO 80214
Telephone: (303) 205-5600
www.mv.state.co.us/mv.html

Connecticut

Connecticut has various locations
Telephone: (860) 263-5700
www.dmvct.org/

Delaware

Delaware Division of Motor Vehicles,
P.O. Box 698
Dover, DE 19903
(302) 744-2500
www.state.de.us/pubsafe/index.htm

Florida

Dept. of Highway Safety and Motor Vehicles
Neil Kirkman Building 2900 Apalachee Pkwy
Tallahassee, FL 32399-0500
Telephone: (850) 922-9000
www.hsmv.state.fl.us/html/dlnew.html

Georgia

MVR Department of Public Safety,
959 East Confederate Ave., Atlanta, Georgia 30371
Telephone: (404) 362-6500
www2.state.ga.us/departments/dmvs

Hawaii

Division of Motor Vehicles and Licensing
P.O. Box 30320
Honolulu, Hawaii 96820-0320
Telephone: (808) 532-7700
www.state.hi.us/

Idaho

Idaho Division of Motor Vehicles,
3311 W. State St.
Boise, Idaho 83702
Telephone: (208) 334-8649
www2.state.id.us/itd/dmv/index.htm

Illinois

Secretary of State, Attn: Driver's Licenses or
Vehicle Records,
2701 S. Dirksen Parkway
Springfield, Illinois 62723
Telephone: (800) 252-8980 or (217) 782-6494
www.cyberdriveillinois.com/services/services_motorists.html

Indiana

Indiana Bureau of Motor Vehicles
100 North Senate Avenue
Indianapolis, Indiana 46204
Telephone: (317) 233-6000
www.IN.gov/bmv

Iowa

Iowa Motor Vehicle Division
Park Fair Mall, 100 Euclid Ave
P.O. Box 9204
Des Moines, Iowa 50306-9204
(800) 532-1121 or (515) 237-3153
www.dot.state.ia.us/mvd/index.htm

Kansas

Kansas Division of Motor Vehicles
915 S.W. Harrison St.
Topeka, Kansas 66612
(785) 296-3671
www.ksrevenue.org/dmv/

Kentucky

Kentucky Transportation Cabinet, Division
of Motor Vehicle Licensing
501 High St., Frankfort, Kentucky 40622
Telephone: (502) 564-5301
www.kytc.state.ky.us/drlic/

Louisiana

Louisiana Department of Public Safety, Office
of Motor Vehicles,
P.O. Box 64886, Baton Rouge, Louisiana 70896
Telephone: (877) 368-5463
www.dps.state.la.us/omv/home.html

Maine

Maine Bureau of Motor Vehicles
29 State House Station
101 Hospital Street
Augusta, Maine 04333-0029
Telephone (207) 624-9000
www.state.me.us/sos/bmv/

Maryland

Maryland has various locations
Telephone: (800) 950-1682 or (301) 729-4550
for out of state calls
www.mva.state.md.us/

Massachusetts

Attn: Mail Listings
Registry of Motor Vehicles
Driver Control Unit
P.O. Box 199150
Boston, Massachusetts 02119-9150
Telephone (617) 351-9213
www.state.ma.us/rmv/

Michigan

Michigan Department of Motor Vehicles,
Attn: Driving Records,
7064 Crowner Drive, Lansing, Michigan 48980
Telephone: (517) 322-1460
www.sos.state.mi.us/index.html

Minnesota

Driver & Vehicle Services
445 Minnesota St
St. Paul, Minnesota 55101
Telephone: (651) 296-6911
www.dps.state.mn.us/dvs/index.html

Mississippi

Department of Public Safety Commission,
Attn: Driver Records,
P.O. Box 958, Jackson, Mississippi 39205
Telephone: (601) 987-1271 or (601) 987-1275
www.dps.state.ms.us/

Missouri

Missouri Department of Revenue
Driver & Vehicle Services Bureau
P.O. Box 200, Jefferson City, Missouri 65105-0200
Telephone: (573) 751-4600
www.dor.state.mo.us/mvdl/motorv/

Montana

Motor Vehicle Division Dept. of Justice
Scott Hart Bldg. 2nd Floor.
303 N. Roberts P.O. Box 201430
Helena, Montana 59620-1430
(406) 444-1773
www.doj.state.mt.us/mvd/index.htm

Nebraska

State Office Building
301 Centennial Mall South
Lincoln, Nebraska 68509
Telephone (402) 471-4154
www.nol.org/home/DMV/

Nevada

Department of Motor Vehicles, Attn:
Record Section or Registration,
555 Wright Way, Carson City, Nevada 89711-0400
Telephone: (702) 687-5505 or (877) 368-7828
www.nevadadmv.state.nv.us/index.htm

New Hampshire

Department of Safety/Division of Motor Vehicles,
Attn: Driving Records,
10 Hazen Drive, Concord, New Hampshire 03305-0002
Telephone: (603) 271-2251
www.state.nh.us/nhsp/contents.html

New Jersey

Department of Motor Vehicles,
Attn: Certified Information,
120 Stockton Street, Trenton, New Jersey 08666
Telephone: Toll free in New Jersey (888) 486-3339
or (609) 292-6500 if out of state
www.state.nj.us/mvs/

New Mexico

Motor Vehicle Division,
Attn: Driver Services or Registration Information,
P.O. Box 1028, Santa Fe, New Mexico 87504
Telephone: (505) 827-0700
www.state.nm.us/tax/mvd/mvd_home.htm

New York

New York State Department of Motor Vehicles,
6 Empire State Plaza, Albany, NY 12228
Telephone: (800) 225-5368
www.nydmv.state.ny.us/

North Carolina

MVR Driver's License Section DMV
1100 New Bern Ave
Raleigh, NC 27697-0001
Telephone (919) 715-7000
www.dmv.dot.state.nc.us/

North Dakota

Driver's License Division,
608 East Boulevard Avenue,
Bismark, North Dakota 58505-0700
Telephone: (701) 328-2600
www.state.nd.us/dot/

Ohio

Ohio Bureau of Motor Vehicles, Attn: Records
P.O. Box 16520, Columbus, Ohio 43216-6520
Telephone: (614) 752-7500
www.state.oh.us/odps/division/bmv/bmv.html

Oklahoma

Oklahoma Department of Public Safety,
Attn: Driving Records,
P.O. Box 11415, Oklahoma City, Oklahoma 73136
Telephone: (405) 425-2262
www.dps.state.ok.us/

Oregon

Oregon Department of Motor Vehicles
1905 Lana Avenue NE, Salem, Oregon 97314
Telephone: (503) 945-5000
www.odot.state.or.us/dmv/

Pennsylvania

Telephone: (800) 932-4600 within state
or (717) 391-6190 out of state
www.dmv.state.pa.us/

Rhode Island

Rhode Island Department of Motor Vehicles,
286 Main St. Pawtucket, Rhode Island 02860
Telephone: (401) 588-3020
www.dmv.state.ri.us/

South Carolina

South Carolina Dept. of Public Safety
5400 Broad River Road
Columbia, South Carolina 29212
Telephone: (803) 737-4000
www.scdps.org/dmv/

South Dakota

Dept. of Revenue, Drivers License Issuance
or Titles and Registration,
118 W. Capitol Ave., Pierre, South Dakota 57501-2000
Telephone: (800) 952-3696 or (605) 773-6883 for
out of state calls
www.state.sd.us/revenue/motorvcl.htm

Tennessee

Tennessee Department of Motor Vehicle Safety,
1150 Foster Ave.
Nashville, Tennessee 37249
Telephone: (615) 251-5216
www.state.tn.us/safety/

Texas

Texas Department of Transportation
125 E. 11th St., Austin, Texas 78701-2483
Telephone: (512) 416-4800
www.txdps.state.tx.us

Utah

Utah Department of Public Safety, License Department,
P.O. Box 30560, Salt Lake City, Utah 84130-0560
Telephone: (801) 965-4437 or (800) DMV-UTAH
www.dmv-utah.com/

Vermont

Vermont Department of Motor Vehicles,
Attn: Driver Improvement Unit,
120 State Street, Montpelier, Vermont 05603-0001
Telephone: (802) 828-2000
www.aot.state.vt.us/dmv/dmvhp.htm

Virginia

Department of Motor Vehicles
P.O. Box 27412 Richmond, Virginia 23269

Telephone: (800) 368-5463
www.dmv.state.va.us/

Washington

Washington State Dept. of Licensing, Driver Services,
P.O. Box 9030, Olympia, Washington 98507-9030
Telephone: (360) 902-3900
www.wa.gov/dol/main.htm

Washington DC

DC DMV Driver Records Office
301 C Street NW Room 1000
Washington, DC 20001
Telephone: (202) 727-5000
www.dmv.washingtondc.gov/main.shtm

West Virginia

West Virginia Dept. of Transportation/Division
of Motor Vehicle Records
Building 3 Room 113
1800 Kanawha Blvd East
Charleston, WV 25317
Telephone: (304) 558-3900
www.wvdot.com/6_motorists/dmv/6g_dmv.htm

Wisconsin

Wisconsin Department of Transportation,
Attn: Records & Licensing Information Section
P.O. Box 7995, Madison, Wisconsin 53707-7995
Telephone: (608) 266-2353
www.dot.state.wi.us/

Wyoming

Wyoming Department of Transportation, Driver Control,
5300 Bishop Blvd, Cheyenne, Wyoming 82009-3340
Telephone: (307) 777-4375
www.wydotweb.state.wy.us/

Insurance Glossary

ACCELERATED DEATH BENEFITS - An option that can be added to a life insurance policy that can provide proceeds to the insured in the event of a terminal illness. Payments are made while the insured is living and are deducted from any death benefits paid to beneficiaries.

ACCIDENT AND HEALTH INSURANCE - Covers injuries due to accidents, accidental death and health related problems. Can also pay for medical expenses and preventative services.

ACTUAL CASH VALUE - The cost to replace property with comparable new property of like and equal value, minus depreciation and obsolescence. Generally, actual cash value is the fair market value of the property at the time of the loss.

ADDITIONAL LIVING EXPENSES - Coverage that will pay for the homeowner to live in temporary shelter when the insured home is temporarily uninhabitable due to a covered loss.

ADJUSTER - An employee of an insurance company who evaluates and settles the claims of policyholders. There are various types of adjusters. Independent adjusters work for different insurance companies, as opposed to being directly employed by any particular insurer. Public adjusters on the other hand, act as liaisons between insurance companies and policyholders.

ADVERSE SELECTION - The propensity of insureds at higher risk to purchase more insurance coverage than those with a lower risk. These higher risk insureds may have to pay higher premiums or worse, may not be able to obtain any coverage at all.

AFFILIATION PERIOD - A waiting period in which insureds have to wait before enrolling in a HMO health plan. If an affiliation period is required, the HMO cannot charge for the affiliation period or exclude coverage of preexisting conditions.

AGENCY - The actual business of an individual agent or multiple agents.

AGENT - A person licensed to sell insurance for and represent an insurance company. Also called a producer.

ANNUAL STATEMENT - A report detailing the financial figures of an insurance company and must be filed with the state insurance department in each state that the company does business in.

ANNUITY - An insurance contract that pays a periodic lifetime benefit for a specified period of time. There are different types of Annuities, each with different payment options for insureds.

ARBITRATION - When a third party helps to decide the outcome of a dispute between an insurance company and one of its policyholders.

ASSIGNED RISK PLANS - Consists of insurers in each state who insure drivers that are unable to obtain insurance in the "regular" market. Also called an Assigned Risk "Pool."

AUTOMOBILE INSURANCE - Insurance coverage for the risks involved in owning and driving an automobile. A typical automobile insurance policy can include comprehensive, collision, liability, medical, uninsured and underinsured motorist coverage and a host of other optional coverages.

BASIC AND STANDARD PLANS - Under HIPAA guidelines, if an insurer declines to issue you coverage after you have applied for an individual health insurance plan or places riders or exclusions on your coverage, after you have had continuous coverage, have exhausted your COBRA or state continuation rights under your group plan. The insurer must provide you with the option of purchasing a basic or a standard health benefit plan and must also provide you with such options if your insurance premium rises.

BINDER - A temporary form of insurance that provides coverage until a permanent policy can be put in force.

BLANKET COVERAGE - Insurance protection that provides coverage for multiple pieces of property at different locations, or for multiple pieces of property at one location.

BODILY INJURY LIABILITY COVERAGE - Provides coverage for injuries caused by an insured driver to someone else.

BOILER AND MACHINERY INSURANCE - Commercial insurance that covers the breakdown of boilers and other types of equipment such as electrical, heating and cooling systems. Also called equipment breakdown insurance.

BROKER - A business that places insurance with different insurers, whom the broker/business has contracts with.

BUSINESS INTERRUPTION INSURANCE - Provides coverage and monetary reimbursement to a business that loses profits, due to temporarily being closed because of a covered peril.

BUSINESSOWNERS POLICY (BOP) - An all-in-one "package" that combines the basic, needed coverages for a lot of popular types of businesses. This type of policy can contain coverage for property, liability, business personal property and business interruption.

CANCELLATION - The termination of an insurance policy.

CAPTIVE AGENT - An insurance producer who is only to represent one insurer or multiple insurers exclusively.

CASUALTY INSURANCE - Coverage for negligent acts, which cause bodily harm or damage to property, for which an insured is legally liable.

CLAIM - Notification to an insurance company to honor a request for a covered loss or peril.

COBRA - The Consolidated Omnibus Budget Reconciliation Act. This federal law allows an employee to continue his or her health coverage under certain circumstances. If eligible, you may be able to continue coverage under your employer's group health plan by paying the full premium plus a 2% administrative fee. You may be eligible for COBRA if you are fired, quit, retire, or if you are divorced, separated, a widow, or a dependent child of a previously covered employee.

COINSURANCE - An amount required by an insurance company, over and above the normal deductible amount, that must be paid by an insured before the insurance company pays a maximum predetermined amount for a claim.

COLLISION COVERAGE - The part of an automobile insurance policy that covers damage to the insured's car resulting from a collision.

COMMERCIAL GENERAL LIABILITY INSURANCE (CGL) - A commercial insurance policy that covers liability exposures of a business, which are not excluded in the policy. Such a policy can include coverage for contractors, completed operations, product liability, premises and operations.

COMPLAINT RATIO - Used in some states by insurance departments to track consumer complaints against insurance companies. The ratio generally takes into account: the number of complaints filed, compared to the number of policies that an insurer has written.

COMPREHENSIVE COVERAGE - The part of an automobile insurance policy that covers damage to the insured's car which is not the result of collision. For example: Damage from fire, vandalism, floods, earthquakes, explosions and theft.

CREDIT INSURANCE - Insurance coverage that provides for the payment of outstanding debt, in the event that a borrower is unable to repay the debt due to the borrower's death (known as Credit Life). Credit disability insurance can repay a borrower's debt if the borrower becomes disabled. Credit card companies and automobile finance companies usually offer Credit Life insurance.

CROP INSURANCE - Coverage for damage to crops caused by covered perils. Crop insurance can be obtained either through private companies or from the Federal Crop Insurance Corporation.

DECLARATION - The part of an insurance policy that states who the insured is, the property address of the insured, the address and location of any insured property, the premium for the insurance and the effective dates of coverage. Also called a "Dec Page," or Declarations page.

DECLINE - When an insurance company decides not to offer insurance coverage.

DEDUCTIBLE - The amount that an insured is to pay when a loss occurs. This amount is required in addition to whatever amount the insurance company is to pay.

DEPRECIATION - A decrease in the value of property due to age, wear and tear, etc.

DIRECT WRITER - An insurance company that sells insurance directly to consumers without the use of insurance agents. Direct writers often sell insurance via the Internet, direct mail and other media.

DISABILITY INCOME INSURANCE - A form of health insurance that will pay the insured during a covered period, while the insured is not able to work due to an illness or accident.

DIVIDENDS - Compensation returned to policyholders when an insurance company has profitable earnings. Dividends that are payable in some life insurance policies may not be guaranteed. Many insurers allow their policyholders the option of receiving the dividend in the form of a check, or allowing the dividend to be "put back into the policy" to purchase additional insurance.

EARNED PREMIUM - The amount of premium due an insurance company for providing coverage. This premium is actually "earned" once the covered policy period has ended.

EARTHQUAKE INSURANCE - A specialized policy that includes coverage for the property of an insured against damage from earthquakes. Most standard policies do not include this coverage automatically.

ENDORSEMENT - Adds or excludes specific types of terms of coverage to a policy. Also called an amendment or "rider."

ENROLLMENT PERIOD - A specified period allowing employees and their dependents to enroll in a group health plan, or make changes to their existing coverage.

ERRORS AND OMISSIONS COVERAGE (E&O) - Covers an insured for negligent acts arising out of the duties of his or her profession. Also called Professional Liability insurance.

ESCROW ACCOUNT - The amount that a lender collects from

a property owner's mortgage payments to pay for the owner's insurance and taxes.

EXCLUSION - When a specific peril or occurrence is not covered under an insurance policy.

FACE AMOUNT - The basic death benefit amount payable to a beneficiary (upon an insured's death) from a life insurance policy.

FAIR MARKET VALUE - The price that a reasonable and willing buyer would pay a reasonable and willing seller, if neither is under any compulsion to sell or buy. See also Actual Cash Value.

FINANCIAL RESPONSIBILITY - The state law requiring drivers to be legally responsible for the damage to property and bodily injury of others. It is usually required to be purchased when a driver is caught driving without insurance. Also known as an SR-22 or SR-22 insurance.

FIRE INSURANCE - Coverage for a property and/or its contents due to fire etc. People will often refer to homeowner's insurance as fire insurance.

FLOOD INSURANCE - Coverage offered through the Federal Government and made available through insurance agents, brokers and companies. Some lenders require this coverage when a particular community is designated as a flood zone.

FORCED PLACE INSURANCE - Insurance coverage "forced" in place by a lender or mortgage company when a borrower no longer has his or her own insurance on a property.

FULLY-INSURED GROUP HEALTH PLAN - Health insurance offered and underwritten by an insurance company.

GAP INSURANCE - An optional coverage that can pay the

difference between what a person owes on their car and what the car was worth (actual cash value) at the time of a total loss (i.e. theft or accident etc.).

GRACE PERIOD - A period in which the insurance company extends coverage while waiting for a past due premium.

GROUP HEALTH PLAN - A health insurance plan that covers at least 2 or more people. It is usually offered through employers, unions and other associations.

GUARANTEED INSURABILITY - An option that can be purchased with some life insurance policies, which offers: The insured can purchase additional amounts of insurance at predetermined intervals without evidence of insurance or having to "requalify."

GUARANTEED ISSUE - A requirement that a health plan must allow you to enroll in the plan regardless of your health status, age, gender, or other factors that might affect your ability to obtain health coverage.

GUARANTEED RENEWABILITY - A feature included in some life insurance policies that allows for the policy to be automatically renewed at future predetermined intervals, regardless of what a person's health status is at the time.

HEALTH INSURANCE - Coverage that pays for medical treatment and expenses. The two major types of health insurance are HMO's and PPO's.

HEALTH STATUS - The medical condition of a person, including his or her prior claims and medical history.

HIPAA - The federal Health Insurance Portability and Accountability Act. Its purpose is to help people buy and keep health insurance, even if they have serious health conditions.

HMO - Stands for Health Maintenance Organization, where Insureds agree to utilize physicians within a planned network. Usually, insureds are required to pay a co-payment amount (as opposed to a deductible) when visiting a participating doctor.

HOMEOWNER INSURANCE - Coverage for insuring a home against covered perils such as fire, burglary, lightning, and falling objects etc. Most homeowner insurance policies also include liability coverage.

INCONTESTABLE CLAUSE - A clause usually found in life insurance policies which states that an insurer cannot cancel a policy for being "invalid" after the policy has been in force for a certain period of time (usually two years).

INDEPENDENT AGENT - An insurance representative who works for multiple insurers, placing business with different insurance companies depending on the needs of their clients.

INDIVIDUAL HEALTH PLAN - Policies for people and their families unable or unwilling to obtain coverage through a group health plan for example, a self-employed person or a part-time person.

INFLATION GUARD CLAUSE - A clause included in most homeowner policies that automatically increases the coverage limit at each renewal to keep up with the costs of inflation.

INSURED - In general, but not in all cases, the insured is the owner of an insurance policy, whom would receive compensation for covered losses. In life insurance policies, the beneficiary could be the owner of the policy and would receive death benefit proceeds, payable upon the insured's death.

INSURER - An insurance company.

INTERNET LIABILITY INSURANCE - Protects online businesses against many perils and exposures related to doing business over the Internet. Such perils could include: network attacks, hacking and copyright infringement. Also called CyberRisk coverage

KEY PERSON INSURANCE - Coverage for a business that provides protection from financial losses by insuring the "Key Person" who is largely responsible for the success of the business.

LARGE GROUP HEALTH PLAN - A single policy offered to a group of employees or individuals who belong to the same organization.

LATE ENROLLMENT - Enrollment in a health plan that occurs "outside" of the normal enrollment period. Also see Enrollment Period and Special Enrollment Period.

LIABILITY INSURANCE - Coverage for damages that result in bodily injury and/or property damage to others.

LIFE INSURANCE - Coverage on the life of an insured person, with death benefits being paid to the beneficiary of the life insurance policy.

LIMITS - The maximum amount of coverage provided by an insurance policy.

LOAN VALUE - The amount of accumulated funds in a life insurance policy that can be borrowed by the policy owner. Any outstanding amount at the time of the insured's death will be deducted from the death proceeds payable by the policy.

LONG-TERM CARE INSURANCE - Coverage that provides skilled nursing and custodial care for insureds, either in a nursing care facility or at the residence of the insured.

LOOK BACK PERIOD - The period prior to enrolling in a health plan that includes identifying any preexisting conditions. Also see Preexisting Condition.

MAJOR MEDICAL PLAN - A health plan that reimburses insureds and/or their physicians for any covered services. Usually, Major Medical Plans do not limit you to a specified provider network like HMO's.

MANAGED CARE - Similar to an HMO, Managed Care Plans normally require insureds to get "referrals" from their primary physicians before being allowed to see a specialist. Coverage is also limited to certain doctors and providers within a specified network. Also see HMO and PPO.

MATERIAL MISREPRESENTATION - When an applicant or insured makes a false statement on an application. There may be grounds for a policy and/or application to be cancelled or voided if an applicant made a material misrepresentation.

MEDICAID - A program implemented to assist people who do not have the ability or resources to pay for health care.

MEDICARE - A federal program for people 65 and older that pays some of the costs involved with being hospitalized, the costs for in-home care, surgery and skilled-nursing care.

MEDIGAP/MEDSUP - Coverage that supplements federally provided benefits such as Medicare.

PAID-UP INSURANCE - A life insurance policy that is paid in full, with no further premiums due.

PERIL - Possible causes of loss in an insurance policy, such as fire, burglary or vandalism etc.

POLICY - The actual contract between an insurance company

and a client.

POLICY LIMIT - The maximum amount that a policy will pay for a covered loss or service.

PPO - Stands for Preferred Provider Organization and is a type of health plan. Unlike HMOs, PPOs typically allow their members (who agree to pay a higher percentage) to go to any doctor. Also see HMO.

PREEXISTING CONDITION - A condition that a person had prior to them seeking health or life insurance coverage. Many policies either charge more for preexisting conditions or exclude them altogether.

PREEXISTING CONDITION EXCLUSION PERIOD - A specific time period after the start of a health insurance policy in which no coverage will exist for a preexisting condition.

PREMIUM - The actual payment amount charged by an insurance company for coverage.

PRODUCER - A licensed representative authorized to sell insurance for a single insurer or multiple insurance companies. Another name for an insurance agent.

PROFESSIONAL LIABILITY INSURANCE - Coverage for professionals offering protection for negligence that may arise during the course of performing their duties. Also, called errors and omissions insurance.

PROPERTY INSURANCE - Coverage for a building or the personal property of an insured.

PRO-RATA CANCELLATION - The calculation of earned premium due an insurance company for the time period that coverage was actually provided. Any amount of unearned premium is usually refunded back to the insured.

QUOTE - Estimation for the cost of insurance coverage and/or an insurance policy based on information supplied by the applicant.

REDLINING - The unfair and illegal practice of denying applicants insurance, solely on the basis of where they live.

REPLACEMENT VALUE - The amount needed to replace covered property with new and similar property at current prices without deducting for depreciation. Also called Replacement Cost Coverage.

REINSTATEMENT - An insurance policy that is put back in force after canceling or lapsing. Usually, a new in-force effective date and policy term will result after a policy has been reinstated.

RIDER - An amendment to a policy to add or delete specific items or terms or coverage. Also called an "endorsement."

SELF-INSURED GROUP HEALTH PLANS - Health plans that are set up by employers to cover the health claims of employees. These plans may be administered by insurance companies, however, are not underwritten by them. Employers normally fund Self-Insured Group Health Plans.

SPECIAL ENROLLMENT PERIOD - The time period in which employees are allowed to sign up for an employer group health plan. These enrollment periods usually last for 30 days or more. Also known as open enrollment.

SURPLUS LINES INSURANCE - Specialized coverage provided by insurance companies that are not admitted to do business in a state. This allows residents in a state to purchase certain coverage that is not available from insurers licensed in their state.

SURRENDER - The canceling of a life insurance policy prior to the maturity date.

THIRD PARTY ADMINISTRATORS - An "outside" company that performs certain tasks on behalf of an insurer. Such tasks can encompass administrative, claims and risk inspection.

TITLE INSURANCE - Coverage for risks associated with land titles, if the land title is not clear and free of defects that were unknown at the time the insurance was written.

UMBRELLA POLICY - Provides coverage over and above the limits of an underlying policy.

UNDERWRITING - The process of determining the eligibility of an applicant for insurance and the rate or premium that the applicant will pay according to the risk involved. During the underwriting process, some applicants may be denied insurance coverage completely.

UNEARNED PREMIUM - The amount of premium that has been received by an insurance company for which coverage has yet to be provided. The premium for an insurance policy is usually paid in advance and is "earned" as time in the policy elapses.

VANISHING PREMIUM - Term used to describe certain life insurance policies that facilitate the rapid build up of cash value. The accumulated cash value can be used to pay the premiums, until the cash value has diminished, requiring premiums to be made again.

VARIABLE LIFE INSURANCE - A type of life insurance policy that offers death benefit protection as well as an investment vehicle allowing the policy owner to put a portion of premiums paid into mutual funds, stocks or bonds.

WAITING PERIOD - A specified amount of time that an employee must wait before he or she is eligible for health benefits. Also see special enrollment period.

WORKERS COMPENSATION INSURANCE - Coverage for injuries and diseases affecting employees that are job related. Employers risk having to pay huge daily fines for not providing workers compensation insurance for their employees.

INDEX

U

V

W

About The Author

Rodger Nelson has been an insurance agent with a Fortune 500 insurance company for the past 5 years of his career. During his career, Rodger has earned many awards and accolades to his credit. He has also written and distributed numerous free articles via the Internet, and contributes to the Insurance Secrets Revealed website in his spare time. Rodger has said: "The best thing I like about what I do, is being able to help people and their families, by offering them honest advice and strong financial protection against the unexpected." Rodger is married to his wife Pat and has two beautiful children: Michelle & Ryan. His hobbies include reading, health & fitness.

The world is before you, and you need not take it or leave it as it was when you came in.

- James Baldwin (1924-1987)

How To Order Additional Copies Of This Book

Insurance Secrets Revealed should be available at your neighborhood bookstore. If you are unable to find this title on the shelf, additional copies can be ordered either through the store, or directly from Trebor and Taylor Publishing. To order copies by mail, send a check or money order for the cost of the book, along with $2.50 postage and handling for one book and $1.00 for each additional book, plus applicable sales tax in the state of Illinois to:

Trebor and Taylor Publishing
P.O. Box 145
Flossmoor, IL 60422-0145

- Or -

You can order securely online at:
www.insurancesecretsrevealed.com

Reader's Notes